ILLUSTRATED TEACHINGS OF THE DALAI LAMA

ILLUSTRATED TEACHINGS OF THE DALAI LAMA

A GUIDE TO CONTENTMENT, JOY AND FULFILMENT

Translated by Geshe Thupten Jinpa
Photographs by Ian Cumming

BARNES & NOBLE BOOKS
NEW YORK

This edition published by
BARNES & NOBLE INC.
By arrangement with
THORSONS
An Imprint of HarperCollins*Publishers*

2002 BARNES & NOBLE BOOKS

M 1 3 5 7 9 10 8 6 4 2

Previously published as separate volumes:
The Four Noble Truths,
A Simple Path, The Power of Compassion and
The Art of Living

A catalogue record for this book is
available from the British Library

ISBN 0-7607-3738-X

Printed and bound in Hong Kong

CONTENTS

PREFACE

His Holiness the Dalai Lama is the head of state and spiritual leader of the Tibetan people. He is also regarded as the world's foremost Buddhist leader and the manifestation of Chenrezig, the Bodhisattva of Compassion.

A scholar and a man of peace, His Holiness the Dalai Lama has travelled the world, not only to raise international awareness of the enormous suffering of the Tibetan people, but also to talk about Buddhism and the power of compassion.

Since 1959 His Holiness has been living in exile in Dharamsala, India, after China's troops crushed a Tibetan National Uprising against Chinese rule in Tibet. China invaded Tibet in 1949-50.

In 1989 His Holiness was awarded the Nobel Peace Prize for his non-violent struggle for the liberation of Tibet. Since coming into exile he has met many of the world's political and spiritual leaders. He has shared with these leaders his views on human interdependence and his concerns about the arms trade, threats to the environment, and intolerance.

His Holiness describes himself as a simple Buddhist monk. In lectures and tours, he disarms audiences with his simplicity, humor, and great warmth. Everywhere his message is the same – the importance of love, compassion, and forgiveness.

The text for this book is taken from a series of public lectures given by His Holiness the Dalai Lama in London,

England, in May 1993 and 1996. The Office of Tibet is therefore delighted to be able to offer these words of His Holiness to a world-wide audience.

In the original lectures, His Holiness the Dalai Lama spoke mainly in English, but also to his official translator in Tibetan. The May 1993 visit was sponsored by The Tibet Foundation, London.

Photographer Ian Cumming's images of landscapes and Tibetan people, both the monastic community and lay Buddhist practitioners, help to deepen an awareness of the context in which Tibetan Buddhism developed and is now being preserved in exile. Rather than attempting to illustrate the words of His Holiness, the images provide a loose accompaniment to the text. For example, an image of a pilgrim prostrating before the Potala Palace, the former home of the Dalai Lama, helps to convey the preciousness with which these teachings and Tibet's spiritual leader are held.

The Office of Tibet would like to thank Jane Rasch and Cait Collins for their many hours spent on transcribing the tapes. We would also like to thank His Holiness's translator, Geshe Thupten Jinpa, Dominique Side, and Heather Wardle for their work in editing the text into book form.

INTRODUCTION

THE FOUR NOBLE TRUTHS ARE
THE VERY FOUNDATION OF THE
BUDDHIST TEACHING

The Four Noble Truths are the very foundation of the Buddhist teaching. In fact, if you don't understand the Four Noble Truths, and if you have not experienced the truth of this teaching personally, it is impossible to practice Buddha Dharma. Therefore I am always very happy to have the opportunity to explain them.

Generally speaking, I believe that all the major world religions have the potential to serve humanity and develop good human beings. By "good" I mean that they have a good and more compassionate heart. This is why I always say it is better to follow one's own traditional religion, because by changing religion you may eventually find emotional or intellectual difficulties.

However, for those of you who really feel that your traditional religion is not effective for you then the Buddhist way of explaining things may hold some attraction. Maybe in this case it is all right to follow Buddhism generally, I think it is better to have some kind of religious training than none at all. If you really feel attracted to the Buddhist approach, and the Buddhist way of training the mind, it is important to reflect carefully, and only when you feel it is really suitable for you is it right to adopt Buddhism as your religion.

There is another important point here. Human nature is such that sometimes, in order to justify our adoption of a new religion, we may criticize our previous religion and claim it is inadequate. This should not happen. Firstly, although your previous religion may not be effective for you, that does not mean it will fail to be of value to millions of other people. Since we should respect all human beings, we must also respect those following different religious paths. It is clear that for some people the Christian approach is more effective than the Buddhist one. It depends on the individual's mental disposition. We must therefore appreciate that potential in each religion, and respect all those who follow them.

The second reason is that we are now becoming aware of the many religious traditions of the world, and people are trying to promote genuine harmony between them. I think there are now many interfaith circles and the idea of religious pluralism is taking root. This is a very encouraging sign.

I wanted to begin with these points, because when I actually explain the Four Noble Truths, I have to argue the Buddhist way is the best! Also, if you were to ask me what the best religion is for me personally, my answer would be Buddhism, without any hesitation. But that does not mean that Buddhism is best for everyone – certainly not. Therefore, during the course of my explanation, when I say that I feel that the Buddhist way is best, you should not misunderstand me.

I would like to further emphasize that when I say that all religions have great potential, I am not just being polite or diplomatic. I have met genuine practitioners from other traditions. I have noticed a genuine and very forceful loving kindness in their minds. My conclusion therefore is that these various religions have the potential to develop a good heart.

Whether or not we like the philosophy of other religions isn't really the point. For a non-Buddhist, the idea of nirvana and a next life seems nonsensical. Similarly, to Buddhists the idea of a Creator God sometimes sounds like nonsense. But these things don't matter; we can drop them. The point is that through these different traditions, a very negative person can be transformed into a good person. That is the purpose of religion – and that is the actual result. This alone is a sufficient reason to respect other religions.

There is one last point. As you may know, Buddha taught in different ways, and Buddhism has a variety of philosophical systems. If the Buddha taught in these different ways, it would seem that he himself was not very sure about how things really are! But this is not actually the case; the Buddha knew the different mental dispositions of his followers. So even Buddha Shakyamuni very much respected the views and rights of individuals. A teaching may be very profound but if it does not suit a particular person, what is the use of explaining it?

BASIC PRINCIPLES OF BUDDHISM

Whenever I introduce the Buddhist teachings, I make a point of presenting them in terms of two basic principles. The first of these is the interdependent nature of reality.[1] All Buddhist

philosophy rests on an understanding of this basic truth. The second principle is non-violence, which is the action taken by a Buddhist practitioner who has the view of the interdependent nature of reality. Non-violence essentially means that we should do our best to help others and, if this is not possible, should at the very least refrain from harming them. Before I explain the Four Noble Truths in detail, I propose to outline both these principles by way of background.

TAKING REFUGE AND GENERATING BODHICHITTA

First, I will introduce these principles in traditional Buddhist terms. Technically, we become a Buddhist when we decide to take Refuge in the Three Jewels, and when we generate bodhichitta, which is known as compassion, the altruistic mind, or our good heart. The Three Jewels of Buddhism are the Buddha; the Dharma, his teaching; and the Sangha or community of practitioners. It is very clear that the idea of helping others lies at the heart of both Refuge and Bodhichitta. The practice of Generating Bodhichitta explicitly entails committing oneself to activities which are primarily aimed at helping others; while the practice of Taking Refuge lays the foundation for the practitioner to lead his or her life in an ethically disciplined way.

Unless we have a good foundational experience of the practice

of Taking Refuge in the Three Jewels, we will not be able to have a high level of realization of bodhichitta. It is for this reason that the distinction between a practicing Buddhist and a non-Buddhist is made on the basis of whether or not an individual has taken Refuge in the Three Jewels.

However, when we talk about Taking Refuge in the Three Jewels, we should not imagine that it simply involves a ceremony in which we formally take Refuge from a master. There is a formal Refuge ceremony in Buddhism, but the ceremony is not the point. The point is that as a result of your own reflection, even without a master, you become fully convinced of the validity of the Buddha, Dharma and Sangha as the true ultimate objects of refuge, and that is when you actually become a Buddhist. You entrust your spiritual wellbeing to the Three Jewels, and this is what is really meant by Taking Refuge. On the other hand, if there is any doubt or apprehension in your mind about the validity of Buddha, Dharma and Sangha as being the ultimate objects of refuge, even though you may have taken part in a Refuge ceremony, that very doubt prevents you from being a practising Buddhist, at least for the time being. It is therefore important to understand what these objects of refuge are.

When we speak about Buddha in this context, we should not confine our understanding of the word to the historical person who came to India. Rather, our understanding of buddhahood[2] should be based on levels of spiritual realization. We should understand that buddhahood is a spiritual state of being. This is

why the Buddhist scriptures can speak about past buddhas, buddhas of the present and buddhas of the future.

Now the next question is: how does a buddha come into being? How does a person become fully enlightened? When we reflect on buddha-hood, we are bound to ask ourselves whether or not it is possible for an individual to attain such a state, to become a fully enlightened being, a buddha. Here we find that the key lies in under-standing the nature of Dharma. If the Dharma exists, then the Sangha will certainly exist – the Sangha are those who have engaged in the path of the Dharma, and who have realized and actualized its truth. If there are Sangha members who have reached spiritual states where they have overcome at least the gross levels of negativity and afflictive emotions, then we can envision the possibility of attaining a freedom from negativity and afflictive emotions which is total. That state is what we call buddhahood.

In the present context, I think we must make a distinction between the use of "Dharma" as a generic term and its use in the specific framework of the Refuge. Generically, it refers to the scriptural Dharma – the Buddha's teaching and the spiritual realizations based on the practice of that teaching. In relation to the Refuge it has two aspects: one is the path that leads to the cessation of suffering and afflictive emotions, and the other is cessation³ itself. It is only by understanding true cessation and the path leading to cessation that we can have some idea of what the state of liberation is.

DEPENDENT ORIGINATION

In the Sutras, Buddha stated several times that whoever perceives the interdependent nature of reality sees the Dharma; and whoever sees the Dharma sees the Buddha.⁴ We find there are three levels of meaning here.

Firstly, the understanding of the principle of interdependent origination that is common to all Buddhist schools explains it in terms of causal dependence. This principle means that all conditioned things and events in the universe come into being only as a result of the interaction of various causes and conditions. This is significant because it precludes two possibilities. One is that things can arise from nowhere, with no causes and conditions, and the second is that things can arise on account of a transcendent creator. Both these possibilities are negated.

Secondly, we can understand the principle of dependent origination in terms of parts and whole. All material objects can be understood in terms of how the parts compose the whole, and how the very idea of "whole" depends upon the existence of parts. Such dependence clearly exists in the physical world. Similarly, non-physical entities, like consciousness, can be considered in

terms of their temporal sequences: the idea of their wholeness is based upon the successive sequences that compose a continuum. So when we consider the universe in these terms, not only do we see each conditioned thing as dependently originated, we also understand that the entire phenomenal world arises according to the principle of dependent origination.

There is a third dimension to the meaning of dependent origination, which is that all things and events – everything, in fact – arise solely as a result of the mere coming together of the many factors which make them up. When you analyze things by mentally breaking them down into their constitutive parts, you come to the understanding that it is simply in dependence upon other factors that anything comes into being. Therefore there is nothing that has any independent or intrinsic identity of its own. Whatever identity we give things is contingent on the interaction between our perception and reality itself. However, this is not to say that things do not exist. Buddhism is not nihilistic. Things do exist, but they do not have an independent, autonomous reality.

Let us now refer back to the statement by the Buddha, when he said that seeing dependent origination leads to seeing the Dharma. There are three different meanings to this concept of Dharma which correspond to the three different levels of meaning of dependent origination.

Firstly, we can relate Dharma to the first level of meaning of dependent origination, which is causal dependence. By developing a deep understanding of the interdependent nature of

reality in terms of causal dependence, we are able to appreciate the workings of what we call "karma", that is, the karmic law of cause and effect which governs human actions. This law explains how experiences of suffering arise as a result of negative actions, thoughts and behavior, and how desirable experiences such as joy arise as a result of the causes and conditions which correspond to that result – positive actions, emotions and thoughts.

Developing a deep understanding of dependent origination in terms of causal dependence gives you a fundamental insight into the nature of reality. When you realize that everything we experience arises as a result of the interaction and coming together of causes and conditions, your whole view changes. Your perspective on your own inner experiences, and the world at large, shifts as you begin to see everything in terms of this causal principle. Once you have developed that kind of outlook, you will be able to situate your understanding of karma within that framework, since karmic laws are a particular instance of this overall general causal principle.

Similarly, when you have a deep understanding of the other two dimensions of dependent origination – the dependence of parts and whole, and the interdependence between perception and existence – your view will deepen, and you will appreciate that there is a disparity between the way things appear to you and the way they actually are. What appears as some kind of autonomous, objective reality out there does not really fit with the actual nature of reality.

Once we appreciate that fundamental disparity between appearance and reality, we gain insight into the way our emotions work, and how we react to events and objects. Underlying the strong emotional responses we have to situations, we see that there is an assumption that some kind of independently existing reality exists out there. In this way, we develop an insight into the various functions of the mind and the different levels of consciousness within us. We also grow to understand that although certain types of mental states seem so real, and although objects appear to be so vivid, in reality they are mere illusions. They do not really exist in the way we think they do.

It is through this type of reflection and analysis that we will be able to gain an insight into what in technical Buddhist language is called "the origin of suffering", in other words, those emotional experiences that lead to confusion, and which afflict the mind. When this is combined with an understanding of the interdependent nature of reality at the subtlest level, then we also gain insight into what we call "the empty nature of reality", by which we mean the way every object and event arises only as a combination of many factors, and has no independent or autonomous existence.

Our insight into emptiness will, of course, help us to understand that any ideas that are based on the contrary view, that things exist intrinsically and independently, are misapprehensions.

They are misunderstandings of the nature of reality. We realize that they have no valid grounding either in reality or in our own valid experience, whereas the empty nature of reality has a valid grounding both in logical reasoning and in our experience. Gradually, we come to appreciate that it is possible to arrive at a state of knowledge where such misapprehension is eliminated completely; that is cessation.

In *Clear Words,* Chandrakirti states that if one can posit emptiness, then one can posit the world of dependent origination. If one can posit that, then one can posit the causal relationship between suffering and its origin. Once one accepts this, then one can also conceive of and accept the possibility that there could be an end to suffering. If one can do that, argues Chandrakirti, then one can also accept that it is possible for individuals to realize and actualize that state. Finally, of course, one can conceive of buddhas who have actually perfected that state of cessation.

The point is that by developing a profound understanding of the principle of dependent origination, we can understand both the truth of the subtle origins of suffering, and the truth of cessation. This is the meaning of Buddha's statement, that by understanding dependent origination, we see the Dharma. In this way we can see the truth of cessation and the path that leads to that cessation. Once we understand these, we are able to conceive that it is possible for Sangha members to realize and actualize these states, and for buddhas to perfect them. Finally, we come to some understanding of what buddhahood really means.

THE TWO TRUTHS

In order to develop a comprehensive understanding of the Four Noble Truths, it is also necessary to be familiar with the Two Truths, conventional or relative truth, and ultimate truth.

So how can we develop a personal understanding of the fundamental Buddhist doctrine of the Two Truths? By coming to know our everyday world of lived experience, we appreciate what is known as samvaharasatya, the world of conventional reality, where the causal principle operates. If we accept the reality of this world as conventional, then we can accept the empty nature of this world which, according to Buddhism, is the ultimate truth, the paramarthasatya. The relationship between these two aspects of reality is important. The world of appearance is used not so much as a contrast or an opposite to the world of ultimate truth, but rather as the evidence, the very basis on which the ultimate nature of reality is established.

Only when you have an understanding of the nature and relationship of these Two Truths are you in a position to fully understand the meaning of the Four Noble Truths. And once you understand the Four Noble Truths, then you have a sound foundation on which to develop a good understanding of what is meant by Taking Refuge in the Three Jewels.

THE FOUR NOBLE TRUTHS

THE FOUR NOBLE TRUTHS
PROVIDE AN UNDERSTANDING
OF THE RELATIONSHIP BETWEEN
CAUSES AND THEIR EFFECTS

Previous
photograph,
a prostrating
pilgrim in front
of the Potala
Palace, Lhasa,
Tibet.

Left, Pilgrim
in traditional
costume, holding
a mala (prayer
beads) at Reting
Monastery, Tibet.

Now let us turn to the Buddhist teaching on the Four Noble Truths. The first question we might ask is why these Truths are considered to be so fundamental, and why, in fact, Buddha taught them at all.

In order to answer this, we have to relate the Four Noble Truths to our own experience as individual human beings. It is a fact – a natural fact of life – that each one of us has an innate desire to seek happiness and to overcome suffering. This is something very instinctive, and there is no need to prove it is there. Happiness is something that we all aspire to achieve, and of course we naturally have a right to fulfil that aspiration. In the same way, suffering is something everybody wishes to avoid, and we also have the right to try to overcome suffering. So if this aspiration to achieve happiness and overcome suffering is our natural state of being, and our natural quest, the question is how we should go about fulfilling that aspiration.

This leads us to the teachings on the Four Noble Truths, which provide an understanding of the relationship between two sets of events: causes and their effects. On one side we have suffering, but suffering does not come from nowhere, it arises as a result of its own causes and conditions. On the other side we have happiness, which also arises from its own particular set of causes and conditions.

Now when we speak of happiness in Buddhism, our understanding of it is not confined to a state of feeling. Certainly

cessation (the total cessation of suffering) is not a state of feeling, and yet we could say that cessation is the highest form of happiness because it is, by definition, complete freedom from suffering. Here again cessation, or true happiness, does not come into being from nowhere or without any cause. This is a subtle point, of course, because from the Buddhist perspective cessation is not a conditioned event, so it cannot be said to be actually produced, or caused, by anything. However, the actualization or attainment of cessation does depend on the path and on an individual's effort. You cannot attain cessation without making an effort. In this sense we can therefore say that the path that leads to cessation is the cause of cessation.

The teachings on the Four Noble Truths clearly distinguish two sets of causes and effects: those causes which produce suffering, and those which produce happiness. By showing us how to distinguish these in our own lives, the teachings aim at nothing less than to enable us to fulfill our deepest aspiration – to be happy and to overcome suffering.

Above, monks going to perform puja (an offering ceremony) at Labrang Monastery.

Left, Chorten (reliquary) beside Langmusi Monastery, Eastern Tibet.

Once we have realized that this is why Buddha taught the Four Noble Truths, we might go on to ask ourselves the reason for their specific sequence: why are the Four Noble Truths taught in a particular order, starting with suffering, continuing with the origin of suffering, and so on? On this point we should understand that the order in which the Four Noble Truths are taught has nothing to do with the order in which things arise in reality. Rather, it is related to the way an individual should go about practicing the Buddhist path, and attain realizations based on that practice.

In the *Uttaratantra*, Maitreya states that there are four stages to curing an illness.

66 **Just as the disease needs be diagnosed, its cause eliminated, a healthy state achieved and the remedy implemented, so also should suffering, its causes, its cessation and the path be known, removed, attained and undertaken.**[1] 99

Maitreya uses the analogy of a sick person to explain the way in which realizations based on the Four Noble Truths can be attained. In order for a sick person to get well, the first

Left, Mandala
in the roof of
a chorten in
Purne Village,
Zanskar, India.

step is that he or she must know that he is ill, otherwise the desire to be cured will not arise. Once you have acknowledged that you are sick, then naturally you will try to find out what led to it and what makes your condition even worse. When you have identified these, you will gain an understanding of whether or not the illness can be cured, and a wish to be free from the illness will arise in you. In fact this is not just a mere wish, because once you have recognized the conditions that led to your illness, your desire to be free of it will be much stronger since that knowledge will give you a confidence and conviction that you can overcome the illness. With that conviction, you will want to take all the medications and remedies necessary.

In the same way, unless you know that you are suffering, your desire to be free from suffering will not arise in the first place. So the first step we must take as practising Buddhists is to recognize our present state as *duhkha* or suffering, frustration and unsatisfactoriness. Only then will we wish to look into the causes and conditions that give rise to suffering.

It is very important to understand the context of the Buddhist emphasis on recognizing that we are all in a state of suffering, otherwise there is a danger we could misunderstand the Buddhist outlook, and think that it involves rather morbid thinking, a basic pessimism and almost an obsessiveness about the reality of suffering. The reason why Buddha laid so much emphasis on developing insight into the nature

of suffering is because there is an alternative – there is a way out, it is actually possible to free oneself from it. This is why it is so crucial to realize the nature of suffering, because the stronger and deeper your insight into suffering is, the stronger your aspiration to gain freedom from it becomes. So the Buddhist emphasis on the nature of suffering should be seen within this wider perspective, where there is an appreciation of the possibility of complete freedom from suffering. If we had no concept of liberation, then to spend so much time reflecting on suffering would be utterly pointless.

We could say that the two sets of causes and effects I mentioned earlier refer, on the one hand, to the process of an

   This is why it is so crucial to realize the nature of suffering, because the stronger and deeper your insight into suffering is, the stronger your aspiration to gain freedom from it becomes.

unenlightened existence, which relates to the causal chain between suffering and its origins, and, on the other hand, to the process of an enlightened existence which pertains to the causal links between the path and true cessation. When the

Left, Monk beside large prayer wheel in Sakya Monastery, Tibet.

Buddha elaborated on these two processes, he taught what is called the doctrine of the Twelve Links of Dependent Origination, or Twelve Nidanas[2].

The nidanas are the Twelve Links in the cycle of existence, which goes from ignorance, to volition, to consciousness, and so on, all the way to old age and death. When the causal process of an unenlightened existence is described in detail – that is, a life which is led within the framework of suffering and its origin – then the sequence of the Twelve Links begins with ignorance, and proceeds with volition, consciousness and so on. This sequence describes how an individual sentient being, as a result of certain causes and conditions, enters into the process of unenlightened existence.

However, if that same individual engages in certain spiritual practices, he or she can reverse this process, and the alternative sequence is that of the process which leads to enlightenment. For example, if the continuum of ignorance comes to an end then the continuum of volitional actions will cease. If that ceases, then the consciousness that serves as the support for such actions will cease; and so on.

You can see that the teachings on the Twelve Links of Dependent Origination are in some sense an elaboration on the two sets of causes and conditions described by the Four Noble Truths.

THE TRUTH OF SUFFERING

THE FIRST OF THE
FOUR NOBLE TRUTHS

The first of the Four Noble Truths is the Truth of Suffering.

The various philosophical schools of Buddhism interpret the word 'truth' in different ways. For example, there is a fundamental difference between the Prasangika Madhyamaka school and the Shravakayana schools in the way they distinguish ordinary beings from Arya or superior beings. The Shravakayana makes the distinction on the basis of whether or not a person has gained direct intuitive insight into the Four Noble Truths. The Prasangika Madhyamikas do not accept this criterion, because they hold that even ordinary beings can have direct intuitive realizations of the Four Noble Truths. However, I will not go into these arguments here because it would complicate my explanation.

Instead, we will turn straightaway to the meaning of *duhkha* or suffering. In this context, duhkha is the ground or basis of painful experience, and refers generally to our state of existence as conditioned by karma, delusions and afflictive emotions. As Asanga states in the *Compendium of Knowledge (Abhidharmasamuchchaya)*, the concept of duhkha must embrace both the environment where we live and the individual beings living within it.

THE THREE REALMS OF SUFFERING

In order to understand the environment in which unenlightened beings live, we must look briefly at Buddhist cosmology.[1] According to the Buddhist teachings, there are Three Realms of existence: the Desire Realm, the Form Realm, and the Formless Realm[2].

Right, Barley
fields near
Phuktal Monastery,
Zanskar, India.

The difficulty here, for most of us, is how to understand these Three Realms. In particular, how should we conceive of form realms and formless realms? It is not enough to simply say that Buddha talked about these in the scriptures — that alone is not a sufficient reason for a Buddhist to accept their existence. Perhaps the most helpful approach is to understand these realms in terms of different levels of consciousness. For example, according to Buddhism, the very distinction between enlightened existence and unenlightened existence is made on the basis of the respective levels of consciousness. A person whose mind is undisciplined and untamed is in the state of samsara or suffering; whereas someone whose mind is disciplined and tamed is in the state of nirvana, or ultimate peace.

We also find that the Buddhist distinction between ordinary and Arya beings is made on the basis of their respective levels of consciousness or realization. Anyone who has gained direct intuitive realization of emptiness, or the ultimate nature of reality, is said to be an Arya according to

Mahayana, and anyone who has not gained that realization is called an ordinary being. In relation to the Three Realms, the subtler the level of consciousness an individual attains, the subtler the realm of existence he can inhabit.

For example, if a person's ordinary mode of being is very much within the context of desire and attachment then such attachment to physical objects, thought processes and sensory experiences leads to a form of existence which is confined within the Desire Realm, both now and in the future. At the same time, there are people who have transcended attachment to objects of immediate perception and to physical sensations, but who are attached to the inner states of joy or bliss. That type of person creates causes that will lead him or her to future rebirths where physical existence has a much more refined form.

Furthermore, there are those who have transcended attachment not only to physical sensations but to pleasurable inner sensations of joy and bliss, too. They tend more towards a state of equanimity. Their level of consciousness is much subtler than the other two, but they are still attached to a particular mode of being. The grosser levels of their mind can lead to the Fourth Level of the Form Realm, while the subtler attachment towards equanimity leads to the Formless Realms. So this is the way we relate the Three Realms to levels of consciousness.

Left, Statue of Jowo Sakyamuni, Jokhang Temple, Lhasa.

On the basis of this cosmology, Buddhism talks about the infinite process of the universe, coming into being and going through a process of dissolution before again coming into being. This process has to be understood in relation to the Three Realms of existence. According to the Sarvastivadin

> 66 **Buddhism talks about the infinite process of the universe, coming into being and going through a process of dissolution before again coming into being.** 99

Abhidharma literature[3] (the Buddhist discourses on metaphysics and psychology which serve as a reference in Tibetan Buddhism), it is from the Third Level of the Form Realm downwards that the world is subject to the continuous process of arising and dissolution. From the Fourth Level of the Form Realm upwards, which includes the Formless Realm, the world is beyond this process which we could call the evolution of the physical universe.

This infinite process of evolution is very similar to the modern scientific notion of the Big Bang. If the scientific cosmological theory of the Big Bang accepts only one Big Bang as *the* beginning of everything, then of course that

would not fit with basic Buddhist cosmology. In this case, Buddhists would have to bite their nails and come up with some way of explaining how the Big Bang does not contradict the Buddhist idea of the evolutionary process of the universe. However, if the Big Bang theory does not entail only one Big Bang at the beginning, but accepts a multiplicity of Big Bangs, then that would correspond very well to the Buddhist understanding of the evolutionary process.

The Sarvastivadin Abhidharma also discusses the precise ways in which the universe dissolves at the end of each cycle. When the physical universe is destroyed by fire it is destroyed only below the first level of the Form Realm; when it is destroyed by water it dissolves from the second level of the Form Realm downwards; when it is destroyed by wind, it is destroyed from the third level of the Form Realm downwards. In Buddhist cosmology, therefore, the evolution of the physical universe is understood in terms of the four elements of fire, water, wind and earth. In general, we usually add space to this list, making a total of five elements. A complex discussion on the elemental mechanics of dissolution can be found not only in the Abhidharma but also in the *Uttaratantra*. These explanations seem to be very similar to modern scientific theories.

Having said this, what is stated in the Abhidharma literature does not always have to be taken literally. According to the Abhidharma, for example, the structure of the universe is

Left, Doorway to building in Dhankar monastery, Spiti, Himachal Pradesh, India.

Above, Khampa
woman with
colorful jewellery
beneath the Potala
Palace, Lhasa, Tibet.

Left, Monk
looking over
the Lhasa valley
from Drepung
Monastery, Tibet.

based on the model of a Mount Meru in the centre, surrounded by four "continents". We also find that many of the Abhidharmic descriptions of the size of the sun and moon contradict modern scientific explanations. Given that scientific experiments have proved these claims to be wrong, we will have to accept the conclusion of the scientists on these points.

So here I have outlined very briefly how Buddhism understands the evolution of the physical universe, or, in a broad sense, the environment. As for the sentient beings that inhabit these environments, Buddhism accepts many different types. There are beings with bodily forms and beings which are perceived as formless. Even in the world with which we are familiar, there are many beings which are perceptible to our senses and some which are not, like those of the spirit world for example.

Generally speaking, the Buddhist understanding is that birth as a human being is one of the most ideal forms of existence because it is conducive to practising Dharma. So compared to human beings, spirits would in fact be considered inferior because that form of existence is less effective for pursuing the practice of Dharma. Spirits may have certain abilities that are not open to us, like certain powers of precognition or some supernatural powers, but the fact remains that they are part of this world where human beings also live. All beings in this world are under the control of delusion and afflictive emotions. In some sense one could say that they are

actually the products of delusion and afflictive emotions.

Lama Tsongkhapa describes very vividly the unenlightened existence of sentient beings in samsara. He uses the analogy of someone being tied up very tightly by the ropes of negative karma, delusions, afflictive emotions and thoughts. Encased in this tight net of ego and self-grasping, they are tossed around aimlessly by the currents of fluctuating experiences, of suffering and pain[4]. This is what samsaric life is like.

THREE TYPES OF SUFFERING

So now the question is, what is duhkha? What is suffering? Buddhism describes three levels or types of suffering. The first is called "the suffering of suffering", the second, "the suffering of change", and the third is "the suffering of conditioning".

When we talk about the first type, the suffering of suffering, we are talking in very conventional terms of experiences which we would all identify as suffering. These experiences are painful. In Buddhism there are four main experiences of this type of suffering which are considered to be fundamental to life in samsara: the sufferings of birth, sickness, ageing and death. The significance of recognizing these states as forms of suffering, and the importance of this recognition as a catalyst of the spiritual quest, is very strongly demonstrated in the Buddha's own life story. According to the story, when he was the young Prince Siddhartha, the Buddha is said to have caught sight of a sick person, an old person, and a dead person being carried away. The impact of seeing this suffering apparently led him to the realization that so long as he was not free of the infinite process of birth, he would always be subject to these other three sufferings. Later, the sight of a spiritual aspirant is supposed to have made the Buddha fully aware that there is a possibility of freedom from this cycle of suffering.

66 **The sight of a spiritual aspirant is supposed to have made the Buddha fully aware that there is a possibility of freedom from the cycle of suffering.** 99

So in Buddhism there is an understanding that so long as we are subject to the process of rebirth, all other forms of suffering are natural consequences of that initial starting point. We could characterize our life as being within the cycle of birth and death, and sandwiched in between these two, as it were, are the various sufferings related to illness and ageing.

The second level of suffering, the suffering of change, refers to experiences we ordinarily identify as pleasurable.

However, in reality, as long as we are in an unenlightened state, all our joyful experiences are tainted and ultimately bring suffering.

Why does Buddhism claim that experiences which are apparently pleasurable are ultimately states of suffering? The point is that we perceive them as states of pleasure or joy only because, in comparison to painful experiences,

they appear as a form of relief. Their pleasurable status is only relative. If they were truly joyful states in themselves, then just as painful experiences increase the more we indulge in the causes that lead to pain, likewise, the more we engage in the causes that give rise to pleasurable experience, our pleasure or joy should intensify; but this is not the case.

On an everyday level, for example, when you have good food, nice clothes, attractive jewellery and so on, for a short time you feel really marvellous. Not only do you enjoy a feeling of satisfaction, but when you show your things to others, they share in it too. But then one day passes, one week passes, one month passes, and the very same object that once gave you such pleasure might simply cause you frustration. That is the nature of things – they change. The same also applies to fame. At the beginning you might think to yourself, "Oh! I'm so happy! Now I have a good name, I'm famous!" But after some time, it could be that all you feel is frustration and dissatisfaction. The same sort of change can

Above, Close-up of a monk in Sera Monastery, Tibet.

Left, Monks on the roof of the Jokhang Temple, Lhasa, Tibet.

happen in friendships and in sexual relationships. At the beginning you almost go mad with passion, but later that very passion can turn to hatred and aggression, and, in the worst cases, even lead to murder. So that is the nature of things. If you look carefully, everything beautiful and good, everything that we consider desirable, brings us suffering in the end.

Finally, we come to the third type of suffering, the suffering of conditioning. This addresses the main question: why is this the nature of things? The answer is, because everything that happens in samsara is due to ignorance. Under the influence or control of ignorance, there is no possibility of a permanent state of happiness. Some kind of trouble, some kind of problem, always arises. So long as we remain under the power of ignorance, that is, our fundamental misapprehension or confusion about the nature of things, then sufferings come one after another, like ripples on water.

The third level of suffering, therefore, refers to the bare fact of our unenlightened existence, which is under the influence of this fundamental confusion and of the negative karmas to which confusion gives rise. The reason it is called the suffering of conditioning is because this state of existence serves as the basis not only for painful experiences in this life, but also for the causes and conditions of suffering in the future.

Dharmakirti's *Commentary on the Compendium of Valid Cognition (Pramanavarttika)* and Aryadeva's *Four Hundred*

Right, Barley fields and village at dusk near Phuktal Monastery Zanskar, India.

Verses on the Middle Way (Chatuhshatakashastrakarika) both offer a useful way of looking at this third level of suffering, and help deepen our understanding of it. Both works lay the emphasis on reflecting upon the subtle level of the transient, impermanent nature of reality.

It is important to bear in mind that there are two levels of meaning here. One can understand impermanence in terms of how something arises, stays for a while, and then disappears. This level of impermanence can be understood quite easily. We should add that on this level, the dissolution of something requires a secondary condition which acts as a catalyst to destroy its continuity. However, there is also a second, more subtle understanding of transience. From this more subtle perspective, the obvious process of change we have just described is merely the effect of a deeper, underlying and dynamic process of change. At a deeper level, everything is changing from moment to moment, constantly. This process of momentary change is not due to a secondary condition that arises to destroy something, but rather the very cause that led a thing to arise is also the cause of its destruction. In other words, within the cause of its origin lies the cause of its cessation.

Momentariness should thus be understood in two ways. First, in terms of the three moments of existence of any entity – in the first instant, it arises; in the second instant, it stays; in the third instant, it dissolves. Second, in terms of each

Left, Woman adjusting the jewellery of her friend whilst waiting for the arrival of the Dalai Lama at Kungri village in Spiti, Himachal Pradesh, India.

instant itself. An instant is not static; as soon as it arises, it moves towards its own cessation.

Since everything arises complete from the outset, the birth of things comes together with the seed or potential for their dissolution. In this respect, one could say that their cessation does not depend on any secondary, further condition. Therefore, in Buddhism, all phenomena are said to be "other-powered", that is, they are under the control of their causes.

Once you have developed this understanding of the transient nature of phenomena, you are able to situate the understanding you have of duhkha within that context, and reflect upon your life as an individual in this samsaric world. You know that since the world has come into being as a result of its own causes and conditions, it too must be other-powered. In other words, it must be under the control of the causal processes that led to its arising. However, in the context of samsara, the causes that we are referring to here are nothing other than our fundamental confusion or ignorance (*marigpa* in Tibetan), and the delusory states to which confusion gives rise. We know that so long as we are under the domination of this fundamental confusion, there is no room for lasting joy or happiness. Of course, within the Three Realms there are states which are comparatively more joyful than others. However, so long as we remain within samsara, whether in the Form Realm, the Formless Realm or the Desire Realm, there is no scope for joy to be lasting. In the final

analysis, we are in a state of duhkha. This is the meaning of the third type of suffering.

IGNORANCE

The Sanskrit word for ignorance or confusion is avidya, which literally means "not knowing". There are several interpretations of what is meant by avidya according to the different philosophical schools and their various views of the fundamental Buddhist doctrine of anatman or no-self. However, the general meaning that is common to all the schools is an understanding that there lies a fundamental ignorance at the root of our existence. The reason for this is quite simple. We all know from personal experience that what we deeply aspire to gain is happiness and what we try to avoid is suffering. Yet our actions and our behaviour only lead to more suffering and not to the lasting joy and happiness that we seek. This must surely mean that we are operating within the framework of ignorance. This is how we experience the fundamental confusion at the root of our life.

Left, painting of dancing skeletons, the guardians of the cemetaries, on the walls of Meru Nyingba Monastery, Lhasa, Tibet.

One way to reflect on the nature of duhkha, according to the traditional Buddhist teachings, is to reflect on the sufferings endured in each of the six "realms" of the samsaric world system.[5] These include the hell realms, the animal realm, the realm of pretas or hungry ghosts, and so on. For some people, such

Left, Lamayuru
Monastery in
the hills of the
Indus Valley,
Ladakh, India.

reflections may spur them to deepen their quest for freedom from suffering. However, for many other people, including myself, it can be more effective to reflect on our own human suffering. Although Buddhism teaches that human life is one of the most positive of all forms of life, since human beings have the potential to gain perfect enlightenment, it is not always that joyful. We are subject to the unavoidable sufferings of birth, death, aging and sickness. In addition, when one reflects on the fact that life is conditioned and dominated by confusion, and the delusory emotions and thoughts to which confusion gives rise, then for someone like myself it seems much more effective to recognize this than to think about the sufferings of other realms.

As I mentioned before, the Buddhist scriptures describe the causal process through which ignorance gives rise to volitional acts, which in turn give rise to a birth in one of the samsaric worlds, and so on, as the Twelve Links in the Chain of Dependent Origination. On this, Buddha made three observations. He said that:

❝ Because there is this, that ensues. Because this came into being, that came into being. Because there is fundamental ignorance, volitional acts come into being.[6] ❞

When commenting upon these three statements, Asanga explains in the *Compendium of Knowledge* that Three Conditions are necessary for anything to arise, and I think an understanding of these would be useful here.

Because there is this, that ensues

Asanga explained that the significance of the first statement is that all phenomena come into being because they have causes. One could say there is an infinite causal chain. It is not as if there were a first cause, or a "beginning" point in time, from which everything arose. Asanga referred to that observation as the **Condition of the Existence of a Cause.**

Because this came into being, that came into being

When commenting on the second statement, Asanga introduced what he called the **Condition of Impermanence.** The meaning of this is that the mere fact that something exists is not sufficient for it to produce an effect. For something to have the potential to produce an effect, it must itself be subject to causation; in other words, it must come into being itself as a result of other causes. Hence we have an infinity of causes. So mere existence alone does not give rise to consequences; a cause should not only exist, it should also be impermanent and subject to causation.

Right, Young man throwing paper prayer flags ("windhorses") beside new prayer flags on Bompori Hill above Lhasa, Tibet as part of the Tibetan New Year festival.

Because there is fundamental ignorance, volitional acts come into being

Asanga's comment on this mentions a further qualification that is needed for a cause to produce an effect, which he calls the **Condition of Potentiality.** The idea is that it is not sufficient for a cause to exist and to be impermanent for it to produce a particular result. It is not the case that everything can produce everything or anything. There must be some kind of natural correlation between a cause and its effect. For example, because the nature of our life is suffering we desire happiness, yet out of ignorance we create more suffering for ourselves, and this is because suffering is the root of our life. The result we obtain thus correlates with its cause.

Furthermore, there are different ways in which conditions can effect a result. These have more to do with the complex functioning of the mind. The scriptures identify five types of condition, such as the objective condition, which refers to the object of perception; the sensory organs that give rise to sensory perception; the immediately preceding condition, which is the earlier continuum of your consciousness; and so on. So you can see that the Buddhist understanding of causation is highly complex.

Let us take the example of fire. What would the material cause of fire be? We could say that a potential exists within the fuel that is used to make a fire, which then becomes the fire.

Left, Young monk with a large pot of butter tea for refilling other monks' cups during morning prayers at Ganden Monastery, Tibet.

In the case of consciousness, the issue is more complex. For example, it is obvious that we need the physical sensory organs for sensory perceptions to take place. Of course, the physical basis of consciousness would also include the nervous system, although in the classic Buddhist scriptures there is hardly any discussion of this, and it is perhaps something that needs to be added to Buddhist theories of epistemology and psychology. However, the substantial cause of consciousness would not be these physical entities. It has to be understood in terms of its own continuum, be it in the form of a potential or propensity or whatever. This is a very difficult topic, but perhaps we can say that the substantial cause of consciousness can be understood as the continuum of the subtle consciousness, although we should be careful not to end up in a position which implies that the material cause of anything is exactly the same as the thing itself. This would be untenable. We cannot maintain the position, for instance, that the substantial causes of sensory perceptions are always sensory perceptions, because sensory consciousnesses are gross levels of consciousness and are contingent on the physical organs of the individual, whereas the continuum should be understood on the level of the subtle consciousness. So perhaps we could say that the substantial causes of consciousness are present in the form of a potential rather than as actual conscious states.

CONSCIOUSNESS

When we talk about consciousness, or *shes pa* in Tibetan, we are not talking about a single, unitary, monolithic entity that is "out there". We are referring, of course, to the mental consciousness which is the sixth consciousness according to Buddhist psychology.[7]

Generally speaking, when we try to investigate our mind through introspection, we find that it tends to be dominated either by discursive thoughts or by feelings and sensations. So let us try to examine how feelings and discursive thoughts occur within the mind.

66 **When we try to investigate our mind through introspection, we find that it tends to be dominated either by discursive thoughts or by feelings and sensations.** 99

Feelings, of course, can be considered in relation to two different dimensions of reality. We can speak about them purely at the physical level, as sensations, but when we try to understand feelings in terms of mental consciousness the issue is far more complex. And although we naturally accept

that there must be connections between the consciousness and the nervous system of the body, we must somehow be able to account for deeper levels of feeling as well, or what we could call tones of experience.

I would like to point out that although very little research has been carried out in this area, and despite the fact that what little exists is still at a rudimentary stage, experiments done on meditators point to a phenomenon which may be difficult to account for within the current scientific paradigm. These experiments have shown that without any voluntary physical change in the body, and without any physical movement on the part of the individual, a person can affect his or her physiological state simply by using the power of the mind through a focused, single-pointed state. The physiological changes that take place are difficult to explain according to current assumptions about human physiology.

There is no doubt that our consciousness and all our experiences are contingent upon our body, so the human mind and the human body are in some sense inextricable. Yet at the same time, I feel that research seems to point to the possibility that the human mind also has a power of its own which can be enhanced through reflection and medita-tion, or training of the mind. Furthermore, it is well known that there is a growing recognition

Left, Rows of chortens outside Testa village, Zanskar, India.

Below, Sangke grasslands near Labrang monastery, Eastern Tibet.

within modern medicine of the power of the will in the healing process. A person's willpower affects his physiology. How is willpower developed? It can be through thinking something through and discovering the reasonable grounds for one's understanding. It can also be through meditation. In whichever way it is developed, it is now acknowledged that the will can effect physical change.

What does this mean? What seems to be accepted scientifically is that all the thoughts that occur in our mind give rise to chemical changes and movements within the brain, which are then expressed in physiological change. But does pure thought lead to such physical effects too? And is it the case that thoughts occur solely as a result of chemical changes within the body or brain? I have asked scientists on several occasions whether it would be possible for the process to begin first with just pure thought, and then, secondly, thought processes occur which give rise to chemical changes, which in turn trigger physiological effects. Most of the time their answers have indicated that since it is assumed that consciousness is contingent upon a physical base (the brain, for instance), every occurrence of thought must necessarily be accompanied or caused by chemical changes in the brain. To me, however, that assumption seems to be based more on prejudice than experimental proof. I therefore think the question is still open and further research is needed, particularly involving practitioners who engage in profound meditation.

The Vajrayana literature contains discussions of the existence of different levels of consciousness, or different subtleties of mind, and the ways in which these correspond to subtle levels of energy. I think these explanations can contribute a great deal to our understanding of the nature of mind and its functions.

66 **It is very difficult for us to glimpse the actual nature of consciousness, which is the sheer state of knowing or the luminosity of mind.** 99

So, as we saw earlier, most of our conscious mind consists either of states related with objects that we have experienced in the past – recollections of past experiences inform our present consciousness – or it consists of some kind of feeling or sensation. As a result, it is very difficult for us to glimpse the actual nature of consciousness, which is the sheer state of knowing or the luminosity of mind. One technique that we can use in order to do this is sitting meditation, through which we free our mind from thoughts of past experiences and from any form of anticipation of the future. Instead, we abide in the nowness of the present,

Above, Nun in
Tidrum Nunnery,
Tibet.

Left, Devotee
spinning prayer
wheels while
performing
circumambulation
around Langmusi
Monastery,
Eastern Tibet.

although we cannot really talk of a "present" consciousness.

When you are able to clear away thoughts of the past and the future, slowly you begin to get a sense of the space between the two. You learn to abide in that present moment. In that space, you begin to glimpse what we call emptiness, and if you can remain in that emptiness for longer and longer periods of time then gradually the nature of consciousness itself, which is the sheer luminosity and natural awareness of mind, will slowly dawn in you. Through repeated practice this period can be lengthened more and more, so that your awareness of the nature of consciousness becomes clearer and clearer.

However, it is important to realize that this experience of the luminosity of mind, of the nature of mind, is not a profound realization in itself. Rebirth in many of the Formless Realms of samsara is considered to result from abiding in such states of clarity. On the other hand, if we know how to use that initial experience of luminosity as a basis, then we can build on it by complementing our meditation with other practices, and in this way it will become truly profound.

So here I have explained how we can look at the Buddha's teaching on the Truth of Suffering. Once you have developed this kind of recognition of the duhkha nature of life, you already have some understanding that at the root of our suffering lies a fundamental ignorance. This, of course, leads us to the Second Truth which is the Origin of Suffering.

THE TRUTH OF
THE ORIGIN
OF SUFFERING

THE SECOND OF THE
FOUR NOBLE TRUTHS

In the previous chapter we looked at the fact that we all desire happiness and wish to overcome suffering, and how, despite this natural aspiration, we tend to create the conditions for more suffering because we do not know the way to create the causes for happiness. We found that at the root of this situation lies a fundamental confusion or, in Buddhist terminology, a fundamental ignorance. This confusion applies not only to the way things are but also to the way causes and effects relate to each other. Therefore, in Buddhism we talk about two types of ignorance, or avidya: ignorance of the laws of causality, specifically of the laws of karma, and ignorance of the ultimate nature of reality. These relate respectively to the two levels of understanding of dependent origination that we outlined in Chapter One. The first level was an understanding in terms of causal dependence, which dispels our ignorance of the laws of causality. The more profound level was an understanding in terms of the ultimate nature of reality, which dispels our fundamental ignorance.

However, this does not mean that ignorance is the only cause of our unenlightened existence. This has, of course, many other derivative causes and conditions, which are technically called kleshas or "afflictive emotions and thoughts". This is a very complex class of emotions and thoughts, described in detail in the Abhidharma literature. For example, according to Abhidharma there are six root afflictive emotions or thoughts, out of which arise 20 secondary types of

emotions and thoughts. The Abhidharma therefore presents a comprehensive explanation of the whole world of thought and emotion.

There is another explanation of the process of being in samsara in the Tantric Vajrayana literature, which details the 80 types of thoughts or concepts which are indicative of our being in an unenlightened state. The Kalachakra literature, which belongs to the Vajrayana class, further identifies the causes of samsaric existence in terms of propensities or natural dispositions.

These afflictive emotions and thoughts, which arise from our fundamental delusion, give rise to volitional actions. So together, delusions and karmic actions are the origins of our suffering.

Generally speaking, afflictive emotions and thoughts are defined as those of which the mere occurrence creates immediate disturbance within our mind. They then afflict us from within.

KARMA: CATEGORIES OF KARMIC ACTION

If that is the general definition of klesha, what is the definition of karma?[1] We should remember to situate karma within the context of the wider Buddhist understanding of the natural laws of causality. Karma is one particular instance of the natural causal laws that operate throughout the universe

where, according to Buddhism, things and events come into being purely as a result of the combination of causes and conditions.

Karma, then, is an instance of the general law of causality. What makes karma unique is that it involves intentional action, and therefore an agent. The natural causal processes operating in the world cannot be termed karmic where there is no agent involved. In order for a causal process to be a karmic one, it must involve an individual whose intention would lead to a particular action. It is this specific type of causal mechanism which is known as karma.

" Karma is an instance of the general law of causality. "

Left, Pilgrim family doing circumambulation around Langmusi Monastery, Eastern Tibet.

So within the general field of karmic action we can talk about three different types of action which produce corresponding effects. Actions which produce suffering and pain are generally considered negative or non-virtuous actions. Actions that lead to positive and desirable consequences, such as experiences of joy and happiness, are considered to be positive or virtuous actions. The third category includes actions which lead to experiences of equanimity, or neutral feelings and experiences; these are considered to be neutral actions, and are neither virtuous nor non-virtuous.

In terms of the actual nature of karmic actions themselves, there are two principal types: mental acts – actions that are not necessarily manifested through physical action – and physical acts, which include both bodily and verbal acts. Then, from the point of view of the medium of expression of an action, we distinguish actions of the mind, of speech, and of the body. Furthermore, in the scriptures we also find discussions about karmic actions which are completely virtuous, completely non-virtuous, and those which are a mixture of the two. I feel that for many of us who practise the Dharma, most of our actions may be a mixture of the two.

If we analyze a single karmic action, we can see that there are several stages within that event. There is a beginning, which is the stage of the motivation or intention; there is the actual execution of the act; and then there is the culmination or completion of the act. According to the scriptures, the intensity and force of a karmic action vary according to the way each of these stages is carried out.

Let us take the example of a negative action. If, at the stage of motivation, the person has a very strong negative emotion like anger, and then acts on an impulse and carries out the action, but immediately afterwards feels deep regret for the action he has committed, all three stages would not be completely fulfilled. Consequently, the action would be

Right, Young monk in the doorway of Samye Monastery, Tibet.

Left, New prayer
flags hung on
Bompori Hill, above
Lhasa, Tibet, as part
of Tibetan New Year
festivities.

less powerful compared to an instance where the person has acted out all stages completely – with a strong motivation, actual execution, and a sense of taking pleasure or satisfaction from the act committed. Similarly, there could be cases where the individual may have a very weak motivation but circumstances force him or her to actually commit the act. In this case, although a negative act has been committed it would be even less powerful than in our first example, because a strong motivating force was not present. So depending on the strength of the motivation, of the actual act, and of the completion, the karma produced will have corresponding degrees of intensity.

On the basis of these differences, the scriptures discuss four types of karma: karma which is carried out but not accumulated, karma which is accumulated but not carried out, karma where the act is both carried out and accumulated, and karma where there is an absence of both accumulation and the actual execution of the act. It is important to understand the significance of this point, and to appreciate that since there are different stages to every act, karmic actions themselves are composite, and their quality can be characterized as the cumulative result of each of their composing factors.

Once you appreciate this, then whenever you have the opportunity to engage in a positive action as a Dharma practitioner, it is important to ensure that at the initial stage your positive motivation is very strong, and that you have a strong

intention to engage in the act. Then, while you are actually carrying out the act, you should ensure that you have given it your best, and you have put all your effort into making the action successful. Once the action is performed, it is important to ensure that you dedicate the positive karma that you have thereby created towards the well-being of all beings as well as your own attainment of enlightenment. If you can reinforce that dedication with an understanding of the ultimate nature of reality, it would be even more powerful.

Ideally, as Dharma practitioners, we should of course try to avoid engaging in any negative actions at all, but even if we do find ourselves in a situation where we are committing a non-virtuous action, it is important to make sure that at least our motivation is not strong and there is no strong emotion involved. Then, even while we are carrying out the action, if we have a strong pang of conscience, and a sense of regret or remorse, then of course the negative act will be very weak. Finally, the action should not be followed by any sense of satisfaction. We should not take pleasure in any negative action we have committed, but rather we should feel deep remorse and regret, and immediately afterwards we should purify the negativity, if possible. If we can do this, if we can live a way of life where we relate to our positive and negative

Above, Mandala in the roof of chorten at the site of the former western gate of Lhasa, Tibet.

Left, Pilgrims prostrating in front of the Jokhang Temple at dusk, Lhasa, Tibet.

Left, Shepherd
at Yamdrok Lake,
Tibet.

actions in this way, then we will be able to follow the teachings on the law of karma much more effectively.

Although there are many different types of negative action, the Buddhist scriptures summarize them as the Ten Negative or Ten Non-virtuous Actions. There are three actions of body, four of speech, and three of mind. The three bodily negative actions are killing, stealing, and sexual misconduct; the four negative actions of speech are lying, engaging in divisive speech, using harsh words, and engaging in senseless gossip; and the three negative mental actions are covetousness, harbouring harmful thoughts and intentions, and holding wrong views. Ideally, a Dharma practitioner should live in such a way that he avoids all these negative actions if possible, and if not, then at least he should refrain from as many as he can. Leading a disciplined life and avoiding negative actions is what Buddhists understand as an ethical way of life.

KARMA AND THE PERSON

How does a Buddhist practitioner actually go about trying to lead a moral life? A person's ultimate aspiration is to attain enlightenment, so one of his or her principal tasks is to gain victory over the kleshas. However, there is no way that a practitioner can directly combat negative emotions and thoughts at the initial stage, so the sensible way to proceed is simply

to find a way of containing the expression of the negative actions of our body, speech and mind. The first step, then, is to guard our body, speech and mind from engaging in negative actions so that we don't give in to the power and domination of our negative thoughts and emotions.

Once you have achieved this first stage, you can proceed to the second stage and tackle the root cause – the fundamental ignorance of which we spoke earlier. At this stage you are able to counteract the forces of the kleshas directly. Once you can do that, the third stage consists not simply of gaining victory over them, but also of rooting out all the propensities and imprints they have left within the psyche. This is why Aryadeva states in the *Four Hundred Verses on Madhyamaka* that a true spiritual aspirant must first overcome negative behaviour, in the middle phase must counter any grasping at self, and in the final stage should overcome all the views that bind us within the samsaric realm.[2]

As we have already seen, Buddhism explains how both the environment and the sentient beings living in that environment are produced as a result of fundamental ignorance, particularly the karma which arises from ignorance. However, we should not think that karma produces these things from out of nowhere. This is not the case. Karma is not like an eternal cause. We should realize that in order for karma to operate, and in order for it to have the potential to create its consequences, it must have a basis on which to do so. It

Left, Chorten at Samye Monastery, Tibet.

follows that there exists a continuum of both the physical and the mental worlds. We can trace the continuum of the physical world to the beginning of a particular universe, and then we can even trace that "beginning" to empty space. Buddhism accepts the existence of what are known as "space particles" and asserts there is a stage of empty space in which the source of the material universe is in some sense contained. In the case of the mental world, we cannot say that the continuum of consciousness in sentient beings is a result of karma. Neither can we say that the unending process of the continuity of both matter and mind results from karma.

If this is the case, if the basic continuum is not produced by karma, then where does karma fit in? At what point does karma play a causal role in producing sentient beings and the natural environment in which they live? Perhaps we can say that there is a natural process in the world, and at a certain point when its evolution has reached a stage where it can affect the experiences of beings – giving rise to either painful experiences of suffering or joyful experiences of happiness – that is the point where karma enters the picture. After all, the karmic process only makes sense in relation to the experience of sentient beings.

So if we were to ask whether consciousness is produced by karma, or whether sentient beings are produced by karma, it seems the answer should be "no". But on the other hand, if we ask whether the human body and the human consciousness

Right, Khampa man outside Hezou Monastery, Eastern Tibet.

are products of karma, then the answer is "yes" because both result from virtuous actions. This is because, when we talk about the human body and human consciousness, we are referring to a state of existence which is directly related to the painful and pleasurable experiences of an individual. Finally, if we were to ask whether or not our natural instinct to seek happiness and overcome suffering is a product of karma, it seems the answer would again be "no".

KARMA AND THE NATURAL WORLD

Now when we turn to the evolution of the physical universe at large, we cannot say that the natural processes of cause and effect are a product of karma. The process of cause and effect in the natural world takes place regardless of karma. Nevertheless, karma would have a role to play in determining the form that the process takes, or the direction in which it leads.

Here we should mention that from the Buddhist analytical point of view, we distinguish two realms of enquiry. One realm we could call "natural", where only the natural process of causal laws operates, and the other is where certain properties emerge, contingent on these causal interactions. On account of this distinction we find that different avenues of reasoning are used when trying to understand the nature of the world or of reality.

For example, in Buddhist analysis we use what we call the

Four Principles. The first is the *Principle of Nature*: the fact that things exist, and that causes lead to effects. We could almost say that this principle implies an acceptance of natural laws. Then we have the *Principle of Efficacy*: this deals with the way things have the capacity to produce certain results according to their nature. The third is the *Principle of Dependence*: given the first two principles, we see there is a natural dependence between things and events, between causes and effects. On the basis of these three principles, Buddhist critical analysis applies various types of reasoning to broaden or deepen our understanding of the natural world. Therefore the fourth principle we accept is the *Principle of Valid Proof*: given this, that must be the case; and given that, this should be the case.

For a practicing Buddhist, it is important to appreciate these principles of the natural world, so that one is in a position to utilize that knowledge to live a life that is in accord with the principles of Dharma. We could therefore say that by living according to the Dharma we would be applying the Principle of Valid Proof, in terms of the way in which we avoid negative actions and enhance virtuous actions.

So, as I mentioned earlier, the

Left, Looking through decorated doorway to large prayer wheel spun by a monk at Labrang Monastery.

Below, Spinning prayer wheels in the Jokhang Temple, Lhasa, Tibet.

Left, Ganden
Monastery as
seen from an
overlooking
hill, Tibet.

questions we now have to consider are: at what point in the causal process does karma come into the picture? and in what manner does karma interact with the process of the natural causal laws?

Perhaps we can refer to our own personal experience in order to answer these questions. Experience shows that certain actions we do in the morning, for example, will have a continuing effect even in the evening. The action will have created a certain state of mind. It will have had an impact upon our emotion and our sense of being so even though it was committed in the morning as an event that is finished, its effect still lingers on in our mind. I think the same principle operates with karma and its effects, even in the case of long-term karmic effects. This is how we understand that karma can create effects which are felt even a long time after the act was committed. According to the Buddhist explanation, of course, the impact of karma can be felt over successive lifetimes as well as in our present life.

At this point I feel that unless we complement the general explanation of the karmic process found in the Buddhist literature[3] with points from the Vajrayana literature, our understanding will not be complete. The Vajrayana explains that both the physical world and the bodies of living beings are composed of the five elements: earth, water, fire, wind, and space. Space here should be understood in terms of vacuum, of empty space, rather than as space in the technical sense

of absence of obstruction. The Vajrayana literature discusses these in terms of external elements and internal elements, and shows how they are related to each other at a very profound level. Through understanding this relationship, our insight into the way karma affects the world is a much deeper one.

As we discussed earlier, the fact that consciousness exists is a natural fact. Consciousness exists; that is it. Similarly, the continuum of consciousness is also a natural principle: consciousness maintains its continuity. To this we must add that in Buddhism, there is an understanding that consciousness cannot arise from nowhere or without a cause; and, at the same time, that consciousness cannot be produced from matter. This is not to say that matter cannot affect consciousness. However, the nature of consciousness is sheer luminosity, mere experience; it is the primordial knowing faculty, and therefore it cannot be produced from matter whose nature is different. It follows that since consciousness cannot arise without a cause, and since it cannot arise from a material cause, it must come from a ceaseless continuum. It is on this premise that Buddhism accepts the existence of (beginningless) former lives.[4]

We have seen that the origin of suffering lies in both karma and ignorance, but actually ignorance is the principal origin.

KARMA AND THE EMOTIONS

There are differences in the way each school of Buddhism understands the nature of the kleshas, corresponding to their various interpretations of the doctrine of *anatman*, or no-soul theory. For example, certain states of mind, and certain thoughts and emotions which, according to the Madhyamaka-Svatantrika and Chittamatra schools, may be considered non-delusory, are seen as delusory from the point of view of the Madhyamaka-Prasangika school. This is a very complex point, of course, and would require a lot of study.

The most important thing for us to know is that afflictive emotion is our ultimate enemy and a source of suffering. Once it develops within our mind, it immediately destroys our peace of mind, and eventually destroys our health, and even our friendships with other people. All negative activities such as killing, bullying, cheating and so forth, stem from afflictive emotion. This, therefore, is our real enemy.

An external enemy may be harmful to you today, but tomorrow could become very helpful, whereas the inner enemy is consistently destructive. Moreover, wherever you live the inner enemy is always there with you, and that makes it very dangerous. In contrast, we can often keep an external enemy at some kind of distance. In 1959, for example, we escaped from Tibet since escape was a physical possibility; but in the case of this inner enemy, whether I am in Tibet, or

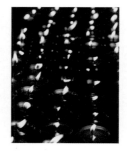

Above, Butter lamps in the Jokhang Temple, Lhasa, Tibet.

Left, Thangka painting of Shakyamuni Buddha, Tibet.

in the Potala, or in Dharamsala, or here in London, wherever I go it follows me. I think the inner enemy is even there in meditation; and even if I visualize a mandala, I may still find this enemy in its very center! So this is the main point we have to realize: the real destroyer of our happiness is always there within us.

So what can we do about it? If it is not possible to work on that enemy and to eliminate it, then I think we had better forget the spiritual path and rely on alcohol and sex and other such things to improve our lives! However, if there is a possibility of eliminating the inner enemy, then I think we should take the opportunity of having a human body, a human brain and a good human heart, and combine these strengths to reduce and ultimately uproot it. This is why human life is considered to be so precious according to the Buddhist teachings, for it alone enables a being to train and transform the mind, mainly by virtue of intelligence and reasoning.

Buddhists distinguish between two kinds of emotion. One type is without reason, and is just based on prejudice. Hatred is one of these. This sort of emotion will rely on superficial reasons, of course, such as "this person has hurt me terribly", but deep down, if you pursue that reasoning further, you find it does not go very far. Emotions without proper reason are what we call negative emotions. The other kind of emotion, which includes compassion and altruism, is emotion with reason because through deep investigation you can prove it is good,

Right, Three young monks in Ganden Monastery, Tibet.

necessary and useful. Furthermore, although by nature it is a type of emotion, it is actually in accord with reason and intelligence. In fact, it is by combining our intelligence and emotion that we can change and transform our inner world.

So long as the inner enemy is there, and so long as we are under its control, there can be no permanent happiness. Understanding the need to defeat this enemy is true realization, and developing a keen desire to overcome it is the aspiration to seek freedom, technically called renunciation. Therefore this practice of analyzing our emotions and our inner world is very crucial.

The scriptures say that so far as the desire to overcome the first level of suffering is concerned, the "suffering of suffering", even animals have it naturally. And so far as the aspiration to free oneself from the second level of suffering is concerned, the "suffering of change", this is not something that is unique to the Buddhist path. Many ancient Indian non-Buddhist paths were similar, seeking inner tranquillity through samadhi. However, the genuine aspiration to seek complete liberation from samsara can only arise from a recognition of the third level of suffering, the "suffering of conditioning", where we realize that so long as we remain under the control of ignorance we will be subject to suffering, and there will be no room for lasting joy and happiness. It may be said that the recognition of this third level of suffering is unique to the Buddhist path.

Left, Woman prostrating in front of chortens beside Tashilumpo Monastery, Tibet.

THE TRUTH OF CESSATION

THE THIRD OF THE
FOUR NOBLE TRUTHS

The third Noble Truth is the Truth of Cessation. The key questions we must ask ourselves on this are the following: What is nirvana? What is *moksha* or liberation? What do we mean by *nirodha* or cessation? And is it really possible to attain cessation or not?

If we were to reply that we must accept that liberation is possible on the grounds that Buddha spoke of it in the scriptures, I don't think that is a satisfactory answer. It may be useful to reflect on a point that Aryadeva makes in his *Four Hundred Verses on the Middle Way.* He argues that when we talk about the ultimate nature of reality, or emptiness, we must realize that the understanding of emptiness is not something which requires reliance on scriptural authority. We can approach it through critical analysis and reasoning.

In Buddhism, we assert that one category of phenomena manifest to us and can be perceived directly, so there is no need for any logical proof of their existence. A second category of phenomena may not be obvious to us, but we can infer their existence through a process of reasoning. These are technically known as "slightly obscure phenomena". Emptiness belongs to this second category.[1]

Since we can infer the truth of emptiness, we must also accept that liberation can be inferred through the reasoning process too. As Nagarjuna says, a true understanding of liberation should be based on an understanding of emptiness, because liberation is nothing other than the total elimination, or total cessation, of delusion and suffering through

insight into emptiness. The concept of liberation is therefore very closely related to that of emptiness, and just as emptiness can be inferred, so can moksha.

On account of this intimate connection between emptiness and liberation in Buddhism, the passage in Maitreya's *Abhisamayalamkara* which deals with the third Noble Truth contains an extensive discussion of the 16 types of emptiness. The fact that liberation is an ultimate truth (and therefore related to emptiness) is explicitly discussed in Chandrakirti's writings as well. So it seems that our acceptance of liberation as a possibility is a function of how well we understand the concept of emptiness.

EMPTINESS

Four Interpretations of "No-self" or Emptiness

When we talk about emptiness in Buddhism, it is clear that we are referring to the absence of something, a form of negation. In the same way, the no-self theory is a form of negation. Why such insistence on categorical negation? Once again, let us pause for a while and consider our experience.

Let's imagine that I have a certain fear based on some kind of suspicion that there might be something threatening nearby. If the thought occurs to me that I may be mistaken, that

Above, Young
monk of Langmusi
Monastery reading
a prayer book,
Eastern Tibet.

Right, Monk
holding a mala.

it may be my projection, then although it will lessen my fear it will not completely dispel it. However, if instead I develop the thought that it is pure and utter illusion, that there isn't anything there at all and I'm just imagining it, and if my negation is that categorical, then of course it will have an immediate impact on dispelling my fear. The question is: if that is the case, what is actually being negated? What is empty of what?

According to the scriptures, emptiness in this example is an absence of the object of negation, which in this case is the object of our fearful apprehension. This does not explain things fully, however, so we have to go further and try to understand what the object of negation actually is. The key to this question really lies in the way we understand the meaning of atman (self) in the context of anatman (no-self). Depending upon one's philosophical interpretation of the Buddha's teaching on anatman, there will be differences in the way one identifies what is being negated here.

Buddhist literature expresses varying degrees of subtlety concerning the identity of the atman as an object of negation. For instance, on one level[2] the atman is identified as substantially real, as a soul that exists within each one of us,

are dependently designated implies that they are not non-existent, they are not mere nothingness. So when an understanding of dependent origination is combined with an understanding of emptiness, we find that this enables an individual to tread the Middle Way, so-called because it avoids the extremes of absolutism and nihilism.

So the Madhyamaka expression "dependently designated" has a deep significance. The first word, "dependently", implies that things and events come into being through dependence on other factors, which means that they do not possess independent, autonomous, or absolute existence. So this first point negates absolutism. The second word, "designated", implies that things and events are not mere nothingness, that they are not non-existent – that they do indeed exist. This part of the expression therefore ensures that the reality of the phenomenal world is not denied. As Buddhapalita states in his commentary on the *Fundamentals of the Middle Way*, if things and events have an independent existential status, and come into being without depending on other factors, then why are their designations dependent and interrelated?

In connection with this point, I have been told by various physicists that they are beginning to have problems in postulating an idea of reality that is in accordance with the quantum understanding of the physical world – even as a concept, reality is a problem. For me, this points to the difficulty of finding essences when we look into the essence of things.

Left, Nomadic yak herders, Spiti, Himachal Pradesh, India.

Right, Young monks
in the doorway of
one of the prayer
halls of Ganden
Monastery, Tibet.

However, if we jump to the other extreme and say that everything is pure illusion and a mere projection of the mind, then we will be falling into the trap into which the Chittamatrins fell, namely the view of total mentalism. So if things do not possess intrinsic reality and yet, at the same time, if we are not happy with the conclusion that everything is a mere projection of the mind, what is the alternative? What is the middle way? The answer given by the Madhyamikas is that things and events arise purely as a result of the aggregation of many factors, and their conventional existence stems from the identity we impute to each aggregation.

As regards the exposition of the Buddhist doctrine of emptiness generally, we find there are many forms of reasoning presented in the literature which are designed to lead to an understanding of emptiness. Of all of these, the reasoning that is based on the understanding of dependent origination is considered to be the most effective. In order to develop the most profound understanding of the meaning of dependent origination, I think the works of Buddhapalita and Chandrakirti are crucial. Much of my own understanding and, naturally, most of the presentation I am making here, is based on Lama Tsongkhapa's exposition of these topics, which in turn is very much based on the reading of Nagarjuna by Chandrakirti and Buddhapalita, to the extent that Tsongkhapa substantiates almost every crucial point by referring to the commentaries of these two great masters.

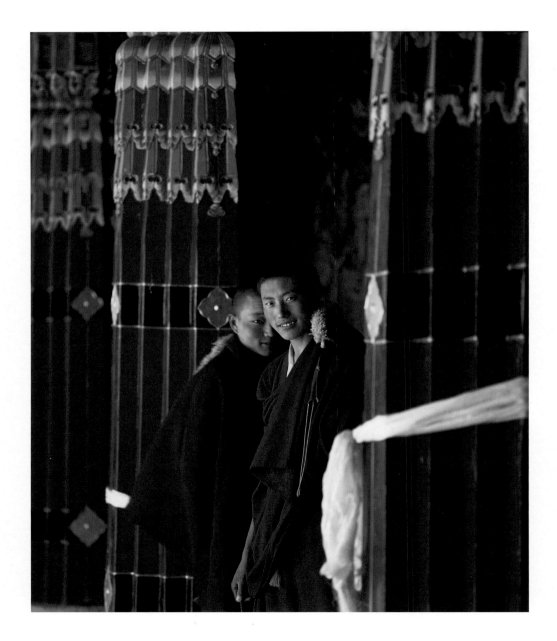

When I study Nagarjuna's *Fundamentals of the Middle Way,* I combine the 23rd chapter dealing with the 12 links of dependent origination, with the 18th chapter on anatman. This latter chapter shows how it is the process of grasping at an eternal principle, or a substantially real soul, that binds us to unenlightened existence. It further shows how negating the principle of atman, and eliminating that grasping, lead to liberation. The main point is to underline how important it is to gain insight into emptiness.

> ❝ **It is the process of grasping at an eternal principle, or a substantially real soul, that binds us to unenlightened existence.** ❞

I then combine my study of these two chapters with that of the 24th, in which Nagarjuna anticipates a number of the objections which could be put forward by the realist schools of Buddhism. The core of their objections could be summarized in this way: if there is no intrinsic reality, and if there is no intrinsic existence and identity to things and events, then there is no-thing. It follows that there cannot be any Four Noble Truths; if there are no Four Noble Truths there are no

Left, Statues of Tsongkhapa in Manali, Himachal Pradesh, India.

Three Jewels; if there are no Three Jewels there cannot be a Path to enlightenment. Nagarjuna responds by turning the realists' own criticism against them by saying that, on the contrary, if things do exist intrinsically then the consequences the realists attribute to his argument would apply to theirs. That is to say, if things are intrinsically real then the Four Noble Truths would not apply, nor could causes produce effects. So the central message of that chapter is to demonstrate that what Nagarjuna means by emptiness is not a mere nothingness, or a mere non-existence. Emptiness should be understood in terms of the interdependent nature of reality: it is by virtue of their dependent origination that things are devoid of independent existence.

Lodrö Gyatso, a Tibetan master from Amdo, captured this point in a beautiful verse.[4] He said that emptiness in this context does not mean the absence of functionality. What does it mean then? It is the emptiness of real or absolute existence. Dependent origination does not entail intrinsic reality or intrinsic identity, but what it does entail is illusion-like, phenomenal reality. So when you understand the meaning of both emptiness and dependent origination, you can posit emptiness and appearance simultaneously, within one locus, without contradiction.

Furthermore, the same master added that all philosophical schools describe their own position as avoiding the extreme of absolutism by talking about some form of emptiness, and

Left, Rock painting beneath Chagpo Ri Hill, Lhasa, Tibet.

avoiding the other extreme of nihilism by talking about the level of phenomenal reality. He pointed out, however, that it is only when you reverse the process that you overcome all forms of clinging: that is the Madhyamaka–Prasangika position, of course. From the point of view of Madhyamaka-Prasangika, then, it is through understanding appearance that a person is liberated from grasping onto absolutes, and it is by understanding the true meaning of emptiness that a person is freed from falling into nihilism.

Above, Mandala in the roof of the chorten at the site of the former western gate of Lhasa, Tibet.

Left, Detail of the Kumbum (large chorten) of Gyantse Monastery, Tibet.

THE MADHYAMAKA SCHOOLS

Earlier I spoke about there being two different understandings of emptiness even within the Madhyamaka school itself, and I outlined how the Madhyamaka-Svatantrika view differs from that of the Madhyamaka-Prasangika. The basis for accepting this difference comes from the writings of Bhavaviveka, one of the chief disciples of Nagarjuna, who subjects the Buddhist realist schools to very critical examination, and at the same time criticizes Buddhapalita's reading of Nagarjuna. Bhavaviveka's own position emerges through these two critiques. In essence, he maintains that although they deny absolute existence, they do accept some form of intrinsic and objective reality to things and events, which Madhyamaka-Prasangika masters like Chandrakirti totally reject. So although Chandrakirti, Buddhapalita and Bhavaviveka were all great disciples of Nagarjuna, there is a substantial difference in their respective understanding of Nagarjuna's philosophy of emptiness. It is on account of this difference that Tibetan Buddhist scholars distinguish two divisions within the Madhyamaka school, which they call Svatantrika and Prasangika.

Right, Monks debating at the Jokhang Temple, Lhasa, Tibet.

These two schools also differ in their methodology. The Madhyamaka-Prasangikas lay much greater emphasis on what is called the consequentialist style of reasoning. This resembles the *reductio ad absurdum* where you are not so much using reason to affirm something yourself, but rather you are concerned with showing the internal inconsistencies of your opponent's standpoint. In contrast, the Madhyamaka-Svatantrikas tend to use a syllogistic type of reasoning to establish their own positions.

Furthermore, there is another fundamental difference between Bhavaviveka and Chandrakirti which concerns the way our senses perceive material objects. For Bhavaviveka, it is valid to say that when a visual perception arises we see the appearance of an objective entity, because he accepts that things do possess a degree of objectivity which is then projected on to the perception. This is totally rejected by the Madhyamaka-Prasangika school of Chandrakirti. It is clear, therefore, that the central point of difference between the two Madhyamaka schools is whether or not one accepts any idea of intrinsicality.

Left, Prayer
flags leading to
Leh Monastery,
Ladakh, India.

APPLYING OUR UNDERSTANDING
OF EMPTINESS

The reason why it is so important to understand this subtle point is because of its implications for interpreting our own personal experience of life. When strong emotions arise in you, say attachment or anger, if you examine the experience of that emotion you will see that underlying it is an assumption that there is something objective and real out there which you are holding on to, and on to which you project desirable or undesirable qualities. According to the kind of qualities you project on to a thing or event, you feel either attracted to it or repulsed by it. So strong emotional responses in fact assume the existence of some form of objective reality.

However, if you realize that there is no intrinsic reality to things and events then, of course, this will automatically help you to understand that no matter how real and strong emotions may seem, they have no valid basis. Once you know that they are actually based on a fundamental misconception of reality, then the emotions themselves become untenable. On the other hand, if your understanding of emptiness is not thorough, in the sense that you have not succeeded in negating the notion of intrinsicality completely, then of course your attitude towards emotion will be somewhat ambivalent, and you may feel that there is some sense in which it is valid or justified.

When you have developed a certain understanding of

emptiness, albeit an intellectual one, you will have a new outlook on things and events which you can compare to your usual responses. You will notice how much we tend to project qualities on to the world. More especially, you will realize that most of our strong emotions arise from assuming the reality of something that is unreal. In this way you may be able to gain an experiential sense of the disparity between the way you perceive things and the way things really are. The moral that we can draw from all of this is that the strong emotions which afflict our mind arise from a fundamental state of confusion, which leads us to apprehend things as real and existing independently. In conclusion, we know that afflictive emotions and thoughts have no valid basis, neither in our experience, nor in reality, nor in reason.

Left, Pilgrim couple making offerings shortly before dawn on the hills above Ganden Monastery, Tibet.

66 **Most of our strong emotions arise from assuming the reality of something that is unreal.** 99

By contrast, your insight into the emptiness of things is not only grounded in reason but also in experience: it has valid support. In addition, your understanding of emptiness and your grasping at things as real are directly opposed to one other, so

one cancels the other out. Since they are opposing forces, and given that one has valid grounding whereas the other does not, the final conclusion we can draw is that the more we deepen our understanding of emptiness, and the greater the power of our insight becomes, the more we see through the deception of emotions, and consequently the weaker those emotions become. Indeed, we come to realize that strong afflictive emotions and thoughts, and their basis which is ignorance, can be weakened, while insight into emptiness can be enhanced.

LIBERATION

We have arrived at a point in our examination where we can conceivably accept that the power of delusions and of ignorance can be reduced, but the question remains as to whether it is at all possible to eliminate them completely and eradicate them from our minds. Some of the points in Maitreya's *Uttaratantra* may be very critical here. According to that text, our potential for knowledge is intrinsic to our consciousness and is an inherent, natural quality of our mind, whereas all those factors which afflict the mind are not an essential part of it. Mental afflictions are distinct from the essential nature of our mind, and are therefore called adventitious.

So when we talk about gaining the perfect wisdom of a buddha, we should not think that we need to create

Left, Preparing
for the arrival of
His Holiness the
Dalai Lama at
Kungri village in
Spiti, Himachal
Pradesh, India.

qualities in ourselves that are not there already, and acquire them from somewhere outside of us. Rather, we should see perfect buddha wisdom as a potential that is being realized. The defilements of the mind hamper the natural expression of that potential which is inherent in our consciousness. It is as if the capacity for unobstructed knowledge is there in our mind, but the defilements obscure and hinder it from being fully developed and expressed. However, once our understanding of the mind is informed by the idea that the essential nature of mind is pure luminosity and mere experience, or the sheer capacity to know, we can then conceive of the possibility of eliminating these afflictions completely.

To sum up, in this chapter we have followed the conceptual approach to the question of whether or not it is actually possible to attain liberation.

Finally, if we accept that liberation is possible, how exactly is it to be understood? In the scriptures, liberation is characterized in terms of four features. The first feature describes it as the true cessation of the continuum of afflictions. According to the second feature, liberation is true peace, the state of total tranquillity where the individual has attained complete freedom from all defilements of the mind. It is described in the third feature as totally satisfying, because one has reached ultimate satisfaction. Fourthly, it is described as definite emergence, in the sense that one has definitely emerged from the process of unenlightened existence.

THE TRUTH
OF THE PATH

THE FOURTH OF THE FOUR
NOBLE TRUTHS

Previous photograph,
Man spinning
prayer wheels while
walking around
Sakya Monastery,
Tibet.

Left, Leh
Monastery,
Ladakh, India.

If we accept that liberation is an achievable goal, how is it possible to achieve it? This question brings us to the fourth Noble Truth, which deals with the true path.

According to the Madhyamaka explanation, the true path should be understood in terms of developing a direct intuitive realization of emptiness. This is because the intuitive realization of emptiness leads directly to the attainment of cessation. However, in order to have such a realization one must have a basis in single-pointed meditation, since this is what leads to an experiential knowledge of emptiness. The point at which an individual attains that experiential knowledge[1] is said to be the beginning of what is called the Path of Connection or Path of Preparation, and the point at which he gains direct intuitive realization of emptiness is called the Path of Seeing.

The experiential knowledge of emptiness must in turn be based on an intellectual understanding of emptiness, developed through inference. Indeed, without that, it is impossible to attain a meditatively-based experience of emptiness. That initial stage of developing intellectual understanding is part of what is known as the Path of Accumulation. The threshold of this path is the point where the practitioner develops a genuine aspiration to attain liberation – and this we consider to be the very beginning of the Buddhist Path.

THE SHRAVAKAYANA PATH

Even before we embark upon the Path,[2] a great deal of preparation is necessary. To begin with, the most important practice is that of the three higher trainings: the trainings in morality (Skt. shila), concentration or meditation (Skt. samadhi), and wisdom or insight (Skt. prajña). The scriptures generally describe the transition from one stage to another in terms of a meditator's experience. It is important to understand, therefore, that the actual path on which the individual travels is that of his or her progressively deepening knowledge and realization of emptiness, technically known as the wisdom aspect of the path. Moreover, the wisdom that realizes emptiness must be developed within the context of the union of the single-pointedness of mind and penetrative insight, known as the union of shamatha and vipashyana.

In order to experience a union of these two, we have to develop shamatha first, for only this will enable us to channel our energy and concentration. Training in shamatha is therefore key. For it to be successful two factors must be present, namely the application of mindfulness and the application of mental alertness. These two capacities themselves will only develop successfully if our single-pointedness of mind is based on an ethically sound life, in which we apply discipline both to our attitude and to our way of life. This, of course, underlines the fundamental importance of morality. So now we can see

Above, Silhouette of the Jokhang Temple before dawn, Lhasa, Tibet.

Left, Monk walking through the fields beside Samye Monastery at dawn, Tibet.

how the three trainings are connected to each other.

All of these practices are common to both the Shravakayana and the Mahayana.

THE MAHAYANA PATH

We must now look at another important aspect of Buddhism, namely the way that the entire teaching of Buddha is founded on compassion. Compassion is the very foundation of the Dharma. The practice of enhancing our good heart and developing an altruistic mind is aimed at deepening our understanding of compassion, and invigorating the compassionate potential that exists within us. It is on the basis of profound compassion that we develop the altruistic aspiration to seek enlightenment for the benefit of all.

Traditionally this is called the generation of bodhichitta. What is bodhichitta? In Maitreya's *Abhisamayalamkara* bodhichitta is described as having two motivating factors: the first is genuine compassion towards all beings, and the second is recognition of the need to attain full enlightenment in order to fulfil the welfare of others. Indeed, to develop the altruistic mind of bodhichitta, it is not enough to have mere compassion. Bodhichitta must be based on a compassion which carries a sense of responsibility so that you are willing to take upon yourself the task of helping others.

Right, Young monk in warm robes at Monlam prayer festival after Tibetan New Year at the Jokhang Temple, Lhasa, Tibet.

This sense of responsibility will only arise if you have generated a spontaneous, genuine compassion which extends to all sentient beings without exception. This is universal compassion. It is called *mahakaruna* or "great compassion" to distinguish it from ordinary compassion which is limited. However, this itself will not arise unless you have genuine insight into the nature of suffering, both your own suffering and that of others. You recognize your state as being one of suffering, then you will also feel a genuine empathy and connection with others. So far as gaining insight into the nature of suffering is concerned, reflection on the first Noble Truth, the Truth of Suffering, will assist you in deepening your insight.

For an altruistic practitioner, it is important to realize that attaining liberation for oneself alone is not enough. Not only is it individualistic, but even from the point of view of one's own path to perfection, it is not a state of full awakening.

It is therefore crucial to nurture our natural empathy and our sense of closeness with others. One of the methods described in the Buddhist scriptures for doing this is to imagine that all beings are your mothers, or someone else who is dear to you. You awaken the compassion you naturally feel for your mother or someone dear, and extend it to all other beings. In this way you develop a natural and spontaneous empathy. However, empathy cannot arise if your emotions towards others fluctuate due to the fact that you view some as enemies and others as friends. That discrimination has to be overcome

Left, Barley fields beside houses near Phuktal Monastery, Zanskar, India.

first, and for this the practice of equanimity is fundamental.

A different method is presented by Shantideva in *The Guide to the Bodhisattva's Way of Life (Bodhicharyavatara)*. He explains a way of cultivating genuine empathy by considering others as equal to oneself. For example, just as you personally wish to be happy and overcome suffering, others too have a similar desire, and just as you have the right to achieve this, so do they. With that sense of equality you reverse your self-centred perspective, putting yourself in others' shoes and relating to them as if they were dearer to you than you are to yourself.

Left, Monks going to perform an offering ceremony (puja) at Labrang Monastery, Eastern Tibet.

According to the Tibetan tradition, these two different methods are combined and then meditated upon. Once you have gained even a simulated experience of the altruistic mind as a result of your reflection and meditation, then the custom is to stabilize and reinforce it by participating in a ceremony where you explicitly generate bodhichitta. This should then be followed by a keen desire to engage in the activities of a bodhisattva. According to tradition, the practitioner formally takes the vows of a bodhisattva at that point. The bodhisattva ideal, or the activities of a bodhisattva, are summed up in the Three Precepts: the first is the precept of refraining from negative actions; the second is the precept of deliberately engaging in virtuous actions; and the third is the precept of helping others.

From the point of view of how causal practices lead to a resultant state, bodhisattva practices are also sometimes

described in terms of the two accumulations: the accumulations of merit and wisdom. The two accumulations come together in the union of method and wisdom and, in the Buddhist path, should never be separated.

THE VAJRAYANA PATH

The profundity and sophistication of Tantra or Vajrayana stem from the practice of unifying method and wisdom. To put it very briefly, one of the unique features of the union of method and wisdom in the Vajrayana teachings is that the practitioner first subjects his or her perception of self and the world to an understanding of emptiness, and dissolves everything into emptiness. That cognition of emptiness is then visualized (imaginatively, of course, at the beginning) as the perfect form of a meditational deity. Next, you reflect on the non-substantial or empty nature of that deity. So within one instance of cognition, both method and wisdom are present and complete: there is visualization of a deity and at the same time an understanding of the empty nature of that deity.

Within the Vajrayana tradition there are four principal classes of tantra according to the Gelug, Sakya and Kagyu schools; these are Kriya tantra, Carya tantra, Yoga tantra, and Highest Yoga tantra (Anuttarayogatantra). The first two classes do not involve taking Vajrayana vows; it is in the Yoga tantra and

Above, Chung-chen bird statue on the roof of the Jhokang Temple, Lhasa, Tibet.

Left, Pilgrims throwing "wind-horses" into the air on Bompori Hill as part of the Tibetan New Year festivities, Lhasa, Tibet.

163

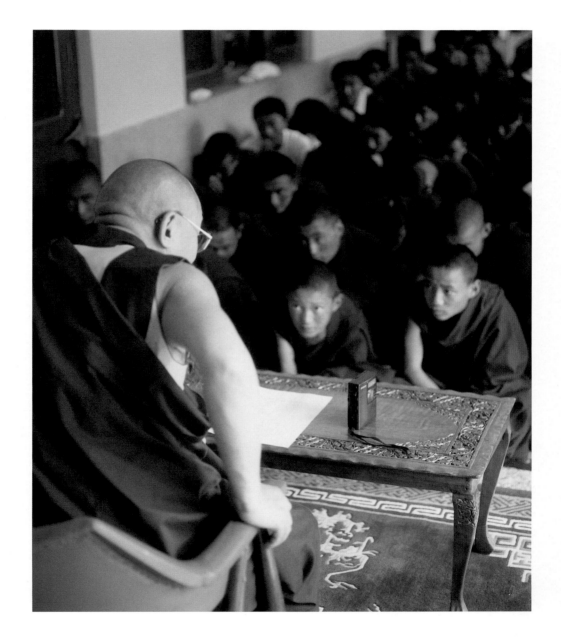

Highest Yoga tantra that tantric vows are taken. The Highest Yoga tantra also has meditative practices which use various physiological elements, such as visualizing the energy channels of the body, the energies that flow within the channels, the "subtle drops", and so on. In all of these various types of meditation the key is always the aspiration of bodhichitta and insight into emptiness. Without these two factors none of them would even be considered to be Buddhist practices.

However, in some very reliable and authentic texts belonging to Yoga tantra, it is said that the Vajrayana path can also be based on the understanding of emptiness held by the Chittamatra school, not necessarily on that of the Madhyamaka. Despite this, I feel that if tantric practice is to be comprehensive, and if one is to attain full realization of the tantric path, an insight into emptiness based on the Madhyamaka is actually crucial.

ADVICE ON FOLLOWING THE BUDDHIST PATH

There are three pieces of advice I would like to share with you.

The first is to say that unless you are able to establish a firm grounding in the basic practices of the Buddha Dharma, such as those I have outlined, then even the supposedly profound practices of the Vajrayana will have no effect. The point is that for a practicing Buddhist, it is really vital to develop an understanding of the Four Noble Truths, and to meditate upon them. Meditation should therefore be an essential part of your practice, and include both shamatha and vipashyana.

Another important factor is your determination. You should not imagine that all these developments can take place within a few days or a few years; they may even take several aeons, so determination is evidently vital. If you consider yourself a Buddhist and want to really practice Buddha Dharma, then right from the start you must make up your mind to do so until the end, regardless of whether it takes millions or billions of aeons. After all, what is the meaning of our life? In itself, there is no intrinsic meaning. However, if we use life in a positive way, then even the days and the months and the aeons can become meaningful. On the other hand, if you just fritter your life away aimlessly then even one day feels too long. You will find that once you have a firm determination and a clear objective, then time is not important.

As Shantideva writes in this beautiful prayer:

66 **For as long as space exists**
And sentient beings endure,
May I too remain,
To dispel the misery of the world.[3] 99

His words really convey a certain understanding to me, and they are so inspiring.

My final point is that the more impatient you are, and the more you want the way that is quickest, cheapest or best, the more likely you are to obtain a poor result. So I suggest this is the wrong approach.

Left, Monk performing circumambulation of a chorten beside Ganden Monastery, Tibet.

CONCLUSION

If I were to essentialize my talk, I would say that if your understanding of the Four Noble Truths arises from deep reflections such as these, then you will gain a profound admiration for the Dharma, which is the true Refuge, and you will also develop a conviction in the possibility of actualizing the Dharma within yourself. On the basis of such a conviction you will be able to develop genuine devotion in the Buddha, the master who showed you the path, and you will also have a deep respect for the Sangha members who are your spiritual companions on the path.

If your understanding of the Three Jewels is based on a realization of the Four Noble Truths that is as profound as this, then whenever you think of Buddha, Dharma, and Sangha, they will come alive for you with renewed freshness. This is what is meant by Going for Refuge.

In fact, to summarize even more succinctly, the whole of

the explanation I have given here is to show what is meant by Going for Refuge in the Three Jewels.

Although my own practice is very poor, very poor indeed, and although I recite mantras and visualize certain mandalas, even so the main emphasis of my daily practice is the Four Noble Truths and bodhichitta. These two practices I feel are of real practical benefit. Sometimes I think that visualizing deities can almost be like a way of deceiving oneself. In my view we must pursue practice step-by-step, with patience and determination. If you practice in this way, then after a year or after a decade you will notice at least some improvement in yourself, and when you see that, it brings a new encouragement to continue. However, we must realize that change is not at all easy.

So now you have read these teachings on the Four Noble Truths, if you consider you are a Buddhist then please put them into practice. They should not remain merely on an intellectual level. Practice and teaching must be part of our life. The same applies, of course, to practitioners and believers of other faiths, such as Christians, Muslims or Jews: whatever your faith, if you accept that faith then it must become part of your life. It is not sufficient to attend church on Sunday and join your hands together in prayer for a few moments, if the rest of your behavior remains the same. Whether or not you are physically in a church or a cathedral, I think the teaching of your own religion must be in your

Above, His
Holiness the
Dalai Lama at
the Royal Albert
Hall, London
in May 1999.

heart. That's very important. Only then will you have an experience of it that is of real value, otherwise it is simply a piece of knowledge in your head and when you are faced with problems in life it won't be of any help.

Once the teaching is part of your life, whenever you have a real problem it gives you inner strength. Also, when you grow old, or have an incurable illness, and when death finally comes, then your practice truly gives you some kind of inner guarantee. After all, death is part of life; there is nothing strange about it; sooner or later we all have to pass through that gate. At that time, whether or not there is a life after, it is very valuable to have peace of mind. How can we achieve peace of mind at such a moment? It is possible only if we have some experience in ourselves that will provide inner strength, because no-one else can provide this for us – no deities, no gurus, and no friends. This is why the Buddha says you must be your own master.

CONTENTMENT, JOY, AND LIVING WELL

66 The basic fact is that all sentient beings, particularly human beings, want happiness and do not want pain and suffering. **99**

Concerned people have asked me to talk about certain subjects and about the best way to deal with the different situations of life. I will try to explain these things in such a way that ordinary people can see how to utilize their own potential in order to face unpleasant situations, such as death, and also mental frustrations, such as anger and hatred.

I am a Buddhist and my whole way of training is according to the Buddhist teaching or Buddha Dharma. Although I speak from my own experience, I feel that no one has the right to impose his or her beliefs on another person. I will not propose to you that my way is best. The decision is up to you. If you find some point which may be suitable for you, then you can carry out experiments for yourself. If you find that it is of no use, then you can discard it.

The basic fact is that all sentient beings, particularly human beings, want happiness and do not want pain and suffering. On those grounds, we have every right to be happy and to use different methods or means to overcome suffering and to achieve happier lives. These methods, however, should not infringe on the rights of others, nor should they create more suffering for others. It is worthwhile to think seriously about the positive and negative consequences of these methods. You should be aware that there are differences between short-term and long-term interests and consequences. If there is a conflict between the short-term interest and the long-term interest, the long-term interest is more important. Buddhists usually say that there is no absolute and that everything is relative. So we must judge according to the circumstances.

Our experiences and feelings are mainly related to our bodies and our minds. We know from our daily experience that mental happiness is beneficial. For instance, though two people may face the same kind of tragedy, one person may face it more easily than the other due to his or her mental attitude.

I believe that the idea that all human problems can be solved by machines or by matter is wrong. Of course, material facilities are extremely useful. At the same time, it is quite natural that all our problems cannot be solved by material facilities alone. In a material society there is just as much mental unrest and frustration, if not more. This shows us that we are human beings after all. We are not the product of machines and our bodies are different from purely mechanical things. Therefore, we must think seriously about our own inner abilities and deeper values.

I believe that if someone really wants a happy life then it is very important to pursue both internal and external means;

Right, A view of prayer flags leading up to Leh Monastery in the early evening light, Ladakh, India.

Left, Monks prepare
to pour the sand
from the Kalachakra
sand mandala
into a small lake
above Ki Monastery,
Spiti, India.

in other words, material development and mental development. One could also say "spiritual development," but when I say "spiritual" I do not necessarily mean any kind of religious faith. When I use the word "spiritual" I mean basic human good qualities. These are: human affection, a sense of involvement, honesty, discipline, and human intelligence properly guided by good motivation. We have all these things from birth; they do not come to us later in our lives. Religious faith, however, comes later. In this regard, I believe that there are two levels to the various religious teachings. On one level, religious teachings talk about God or the Almighty, or, in Buddhism, about Nirvana and the next life. Yet on a different level, all religious teachings and traditions teach us to be good human beings, to be warmhearted people. These religious teachings simply strengthen the basic human good qualities which we have from birth.

As humans, we all have the same human potential, unless there is some sort of retarded brain function. The wonderful human brain is the source of our strength and the source of our future, provided we utilize it in the right direction. If we use the brilliant human mind in the wrong way, it is really a disaster. I think human beings are the superior sentient beings on this planet. Humans have the potential not only to create happy lives for themselves, but also to help other beings. We have a natural creative quality and it is very important to realize this.

It is my belief that the human brain and basic human compassion are by nature in some kind of balance. Sometimes,

when we grow up, we may neglect human affection and simply concentrate on the human brain, thus losing the balance. It is then that disasters and unwelcome things happen. If we look at different species of mammals, we will see that nature is very important and that it is a forceful factor that creates some sort of balanced way.

Right, Monks at the Kalachakra Initiation ceremony, Ki Monastery, Spiti, India.

66 **With realization of one's own potential and self-confidence in one's ability, one can build a better world.** 99

With the realization of one's own potential and self-confidence in one's ability, one can build a better world. According to my own experience, self-confidence is very important. That sort of confidence is not a blind one; it is an awareness of one's own potential. On that basis, human beings can transform themselves by increasing the good qualities and reducing the negative qualities. Transformation does not mean 100 percent change. Without a basis of something to aim for, how do we develop good things? Buddhists call this potential "Buddha Nature," which is also the fundamental Clear Light nature of the mind.

Above, Prayer wheels spinning at Tashikhyil Monastery, Amdo, Eastern Tibet.

Right, Monk walking in the hills above Ki Monastery, Spiti, India.

The fundamental teaching of the Buddha is his teaching on the Four Noble Truths: 1) That there is suffering; 2) that suffering has cause; 3) that there is cessation of suffering; and, 4) that there is a path to such freedom. The underlying principle of this teaching is the universal principle of causality. What becomes important in the understanding of this basic teaching is a genuine awareness of one's own potentials and the need to utilize them to their fullest. Seen in this light, every human action becomes significant.

For example, the smile is a very important feature of the human face. But because of human intelligence, even that good part of human nature can be used in the wrong way, such as sarcastic smiles or diplomatic smiles, which only serve to create suspicion. I feel that a genuine, affectionate smile is very important in our day-to-day lives. How one creates that smile largely depends on one's own attitude. It is illogical to expect smiles from others if one does not smile oneself. Therefore, one can see that many things depend on one's own behavior.

Now we should talk about our motivation and mental attitude. As I mentioned earlier, the facility which can provide positive things also has the potential for negative things. The important thing is to use human intelligence and judgment,

and to be mindful of the benefits for long-term and short-term happiness. Up to a certain point, the body itself is a good indicator. For instance, if some sort of food causes you discomfort one day, then later you will not want to consume that type of food. It seems that at a certain stage the body itself can tell us what is suitable for our well-being and happiness and what is not. For example, on certain days we tend to have a greater wish to eat green salads and certain vegetables, while on other days we may wish to have something else. In a way, these are bodily indications pointing out what is conducive to our constitution and what is not.

While it is very clear, for instance, that when our bodies need more liquid we develop thirst, sometimes our bodies' indications may be confusing. In those instances it is the responsibility of human intelligence to judge what is best. Sometimes your intelligence may oppose your immediate desire because it knows the long-term consequences. Thus, the role of intelligence is to determine the positive and negative potential of an event or factor which could have both positive and negative results. It is the role of intelligence, with the full awareness that is provided by education, to judge and accordingly utilize the potential for one's own benefit or well-being.

If we examine our mental world, we find that there are various mental factors which have both positive and negative aspects. For instance, we can look at two types of mental

Right, Young layman in traditional Amdo dress, Ganja grasslands, Amdo, Eastern Tibet.

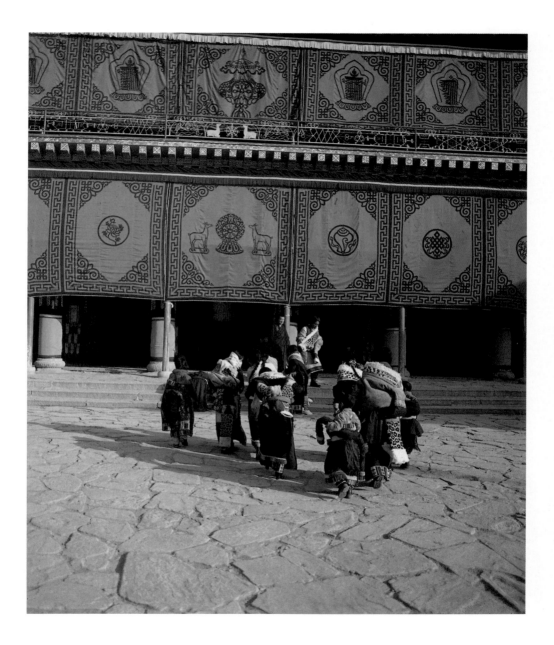

factors which are quite similar: one is self-confidence and the other is conceit or pride. Both of them are similar in that they are uplifting states of mind which give you a certain degree of confidence and boldness. But conceit and pride tend to lead to more negative consequences, whereas self-confidence tends to lead to more positive consequences. I usually make a distinction between different types of ego. One type of ego is self-cherishing in order to get some benefit for itself, disregarding the rights of others and even taking advantage of others with acts such as killing, stealing, and so on. This is the negative ego. Another ego says, "I must be a good human being. I must serve. I must take full responsibility." That kind of strong feeling of "I" or self opposes some of our negative emotions. Unless you have a strong feeling of self-confidence based on a strong self, it is very difficult to do battle with these negative emotions. So there are two types of ego, and wisdom or intelligence makes a distinction. Similarly, we must be able to distinguish between genuine humility and a lack of confidence. One may confuse the two because both of these are sort of slightly humbling mental functions, but one is positive and the other is negative.

" Attachment tends to lead to negative consequences, whereas love and compassion lead to positive consequences. "

Right, A view of
Dhankar Monastery
in the late after-
noon, dramatically
perched on a ridge
in the Spiti valley,
India.

Another example of this may be seen if we examine lov-ingkindness and compassion on the one hand, and strong attachment on the other. While both are concerned with an object of endearment, strong attachment tends to lead to negative consequences, whereas love and compassion lead to more positive consequences. Thus two states of mind which show the same basic characteristics can have differing nega-tive and positive results.

Desire is the same. There is both positive and negative desire. I think generally that desire which has proper reasons is positive, whereas desire which has no proper reasons is negative and can lead to problems. Desire is the prime mover in achieving happiness now and for the future. From the Buddhist viewpoint, the attainment of Buddhahood can be achieved only through a certain type of desire. For instance, the Mahayana Buddhist literature mentions two desires or two aspirations. One is the aspiration to be of benefit to all sentient beings and the other is the aspiration to attain fully the Enlightened state for that purpose. Without these two types of aspiration, the attainment of full Enlightenment is not possible. But there are also negative things which result from desire. The antidote to this negative desire is content-ment. There are always extremes, but the middle way is the proper way. So if desire pushes you toward the extreme, then your intelligence has the responsibility to check that course and return you to the center.

The sense of contentment is a key factor for attaining happiness. Bodily health, material wealth, and companions and friends are three factors for happiness. Contentment is the key that will determine the outcome of your relations with all three of these factors.

First, with regard to the body, one can see that too much attachment to one's own body sometimes leads to problems. For that reason, Buddhist training looks at the body from a different angle and tries to analyze the nature of the body. To me, thinking along these lines is very useful. I think about the source of my body and the very nature of blood, bones, and flesh. The body is not something pure. Even the act of birth is bloody. Also, no matter how beautiful or polished your body appears on the outside, inside there are still a lot of dirty things. With the covering of skin, the human body sometimes looks very beautiful. But if you look more closely, then this body is really quite horrible! Even though we consume good food, with a nice color, taste, and smell, the food is transformed into dirty things. Yet if we try to remove these dirty aspects of the body we cannot survive. And this is the case not only for other people's bodies, but one's own body too. Most importantly, it is because of our bodies that we have illness, old age, pain, and death. Yet despite these faults, the body is very precious because of intelligence, which we can use for many great works. Thus, when one's desire or attachment to one's body becomes extreme, it is very effective to meditate on

Left, A Young monk practicing a sacred dance at Tashikhyil Monastery, Amdo, Eastern Tibet.

191

the impure aspects of the body, particularly to reflect on its source, its constitution and its functions, so that one will have a more realistic and moderate outlook on the body.

Similarly, when our attitude toward our material possessions and wealth is not proper, it can lead to an extreme attachment toward such things as our property, houses, and belongings. This can lead to an inability to feel contented. If that happens, then one will always remain in a state of dissatisfaction, always wanting more. In a way, one is then really poor, because the suffering of poverty is the suffering of wanting something and feeling the lack of it. So even though one may have a lot of material possessions, if one is mentally poor, then one will always feel lacking and will always want more.

On the other hand, material facilities are quite crucial for society, because when individuals acquire material possessions and develop materially, it contributes in a way to the well-being of the society and the community. For that you need a certain degree of what I would call healthy competition, because without competition perhaps there might not be such good progress and material development. But it is still quite important to be aware of what type of competition we need, which is a sort of friendly competition that would not seek the destruction or the downfall of rivals or other people, but rather would act as a stimulating factor for growth and progress.

Personally, I can see some parallels between the need for competition in material development and spiritual development in

Above, Monks with a ceremonial parasol going to prayers at Tashikhyil Monastery.

Buddhism. In Buddhism, the foundation of the path is taking refuge in the Three Jewels: the Buddha, the Dharma and the sangha (the spiritual community). The Buddha, being a fully Enlightened being, is very difficult to emulate. You may draw inspiration from the example of the Buddha, but you can't really compete with him, whereas when you take refuge in the sangha, the spiritual community, within the community there may be spiritual companions who are at the very beginning of the path to Enlightenment. When you reflect upon the qualities of the sangha, then you can get a sense of encouragement – you feel as if you can compete with the others. This is not really a negative competition; it is a healthy competition. Also, you can emulate the example of others ahead of you, with the confidence that you can reach their stage.

Now when we talk about objects of enjoyment or desire and material well-being, Buddhist literature mentions five types of object of desire: form, sound, odors, tastes, and tactile sensations. Whether or not these objects of enjoyment give rise to happiness, satisfaction, and contentment, or, conversely, give rise to suffering and dissatisfaction depends very much on how you apply your faculty of intelligence.

Similarly, just as in the case of material objects, one's

Left, Fires of juniper incense burning on hilltops at dawn beside Nechung Monastery, Tibet.

relations to one's friends and companions have different potentials. In some cases, a certain type of interaction with one's friends or companions could lead to additional suffering, frustration and dissatisfaction. A certain type of interaction can also lead to satisfaction, a sense of fulfillment, and happiness. Again, the outcome of our interactions depends upon the application of intelligence.

Another important issue is sexual relations. Sexual relations are part of nature and without them there would be no more human beings – that is clear. But to go to the extreme, to a sort of blind love, often creates problems and more misery. I think the main purpose of sexual relations is reproduction, the creation of beautiful new young babies. One must not have just the desire for sexual pleasure, but also a sense of responsibility, a sense of commitment. If we look at other species, I think some are very admirable. For example, certain birds, such as swans, base their relationships solely on a sense of responsibility and they mate for life. This is very beautiful! Some other animals, like dogs, do not have that kind of responsibility and just enjoy the sexual act, leaving the mother with the entire responsibility. This, I think, is awful!

I think as human beings we must follow nature, but the more civilized manner for sexual relations is not just to seek temporary satisfaction. If one does not see the sense of responsibility and marriage, this is short-sighted. Sometimes people ask me about marriage. Of course I have no experience

Right, Pilgrims and a monk turning prayer wheels at Tashikhyil Monastery, Amdo, Eastern Tibet with a large chorten (reliquary) in the background.

of it, but I am quite sure about one thing: marriage with too much haste is dangerous. First you must have a long period to examine one another and afterwards, when you have genuine confidence that you can live together, then you should marry. That is the proper way.

It seems that many families in these modern times have problems. One reason is that sexual freedom is too extreme. Moreover, part of your modern culture promotes sex and sexual things and I think this is not very healthy. On the other hand, if we compare sex with violence, then I think sex is better! But often because of sex, violence is also created. I think in reality they are very interlinked.

While the most important thing in family life is children, birth control is also extremely important. Of course, from the Buddhist viewpoint, each individual human life is very precious. From that viewpoint, birth control is not good. But at the same time, the world's population is simply getting too great. Perhaps five billion people can be sustained if all the natural resources are utilized properly, and, according to some scientists, another two or three billion more may be acceptable. But I think it is better if we have a smaller number of people; this is more peaceful and more friendly. With this larger interest then, the conclusion is quite clear that we have to use birth control for the benefit of all humanity. Birth control is very necessary.

So, to repeat, our behavior in our daily lives is the key factor in determining whether all these facilities and relations

Left, A row of standing ritual bells and scepters (vajras) on an altar, which symbolize the union of wisdom (bell) and method (vajra).

really produce genuine, long-lasting satisfaction or not. Much depends on our own attitude. And for this mental factor, motivation is the key thing.

In Buddhist literature, human life is seen as a favorable form of existence or rebirth. There are various factors that could complement the favorable existence as a human being, such as having a long life, good health, material possessions, and eloquence so that one can relate to others in a more beneficial way. But as I pointed out earlier, whether or not these conditions can lead to a more beneficial existence or to a more harmful one depends very much on how you utilize them and whether or not you apply the faculty of intelligence.

On that point, Buddhist literature mentions the practice of the Six Perfections. For instance, in the case of acquiring material possessions, according to Buddhism, generosity and the act of giving are seen as causes of wealth. But in order to practice generosity and giving successfully, one must first of all have a sound ethical discipline, a certain type of outlook, and principles. And that ethical discipline or those principles can come about only if one has the ability to bear hardships and adverse circumstances when confronted with them. For that, you also need a certain degree of exertion or joyful effort. In order to practice the application of joyful effort successfully, one must have the ability to concentrate, to focus on events, actions, or goals. That in turn depends on whether or not you have the ability to exercise your power of judgment, to judge between what is desirable and

what is undesirable, what is negative and what is positive. So, in a way, all these Six Perfections are related to the acquisition of even one of the conditions, say, material wealth.

> **Swans base their relationships solely on responsibility and they mate for life. This is beautiful.**

How do we go about implementing in our daily lives the principles which are stipulated in the practice of the Six Perfections? Buddhism recommends living one's life within the ethical discipline of observance of what are known as the Ten Precepts, or Avoidance of the Ten Negative Actions. Out of these Ten Negative Actions, one, known as "wrong views" or "perverted views," might make more sense within the context of a religious belief. Other than that, all the other nine Negative Actions are, I would say, common denominators of all religious traditions. They are seen as negative or undesirable for society in general, regardless of any religious point of view.

To conclude, good conduct is the way in which life becomes more meaningful, more constructive, and more peaceful. For this, much depends on our own behavior and our own mental attitude.

Left, Monks walk past a colorful banner beside a building in Tashikhyil Monastery, Amdo, Eastern Tibet.

FACING DEATH
AND DYING WELL

Left, A painting of the Tibetan Wheel of Life on the wall of the Norbulingka Institute, Dharamsala, India.

The issue of facing death in a peaceful manner is a very difficult one. According to common sense, there seems to be two ways of dealing with the problem and the suffering. The first is simply to try to avoid the problem, to put it out of your mind, even though the reality of that problem is still there and it is not minimized. Another way of dealing with this issue is to look directly at the problem and analyze it, make it familiar to you and make it clear that it is a part of all our lives.

I have already touched on the topic of the body and illness. Illness happens. It is not something exceptional; it is part of nature and a fact of life. It happens because the body is there. Of course we have every right to avoid illness and pain, but in spite of that effort, when illness happens it is better to accept it. While you should make every effort to cure it as soon as possible, you should have no extra mental burden. As the great Indian scholar Shantideva has said: "If there is a way to overcome the suffering, then there is no need to worry; if there is no way to overcome the suffering, then there is no use in worrying." That kind of rational attitude is quite useful.

Now I want to speak about death. Death is a part of all our lives. Whether we like it or not, it is bound to happen. Instead of avoiding thinking about it, it is better to understand its meaning. On the news we often see murders and death, but some people seem to think that death happens only to others, not to themselves. That kind of attitude is wrong. We all have the same body, the same human flesh, and therefore we will all die. There is a big difference, of course, between natural death and accidental death, but basically death will come sooner or later. If from the beginning your attitude is, "Yes, death is part of our lives," then it may be easier to face. So there are two distinct approaches to dealing with a problem. One is to simply avoid it by not thinking about it. The other, which is much more effective, is to face it directly so that you are already conscious of it. Generally, there are two types of problem or suffering: with one type, it is possible that, by adopting a certain attitude, one will be able to actually reduce the force and level of suffering and anxiety. However, there could be other types of problem and suffering for which adopting a certain type of attitude and way of thinking may not necessarily reduce the level of suffering, but which would still prepare you to face it.

6 6 **The success of our lives and our futures depends on our individual motivation and determination.** 9 9

When unfortunate things happen in our lives there are two possible results. One possibility is mental unrest, anxiety, fear,

doubt, frustration, and eventually depression, and, in the worst case, even suicide. That's one way. The other possibility is that because of that tragic experience you become more realistic, you become closer to reality. With the power of investigation, the tragic experience may make you stronger and increase your self-confidence and self-reliance. The unfortunate event can be a source of inner strength.

The success of our lives and our futures, as I have said, depends on our individual motivation and determination or self-confidence. Through difficult experiences, life sometimes becomes more meaningful. If you look at people who, from the beginning of their lives, have had everything, you may see that when small things happen they soon lose hope or grow irritated. Others, like the generation of people in England who experienced World War II, have developed stronger mental attitudes as a result of their hardships. I think the person who has had more experience of hardships can stand more firmly in the face of problems than the person who has never experienced suffering. From this angle then, some suffering can be a good lesson for life.

Now is this attitude just a way of deceiving oneself? Personally, I have lost my country and, worse still, in my country there has been a lot of destruction, suffering, and unhappiness. I have spent not only the majority of my life but also the best part of my life outside Tibet. If you think of this from that angle alone, there is hardly anything that is positive. But from another angle, you can see that because of these unfortunate things I have had another type of freedom, such as the opportunity of meeting different people from different traditions, and also of meeting scientists from different fields. From those experiences my life has been enriched and I have learned many valuable things. So my tragic experiences have also had some valuable aspects.

Looking at problems from these different angles actually lessens the mental burden or mental frustration. From the Buddhist viewpoint, every event has many aspects, and naturally, one event can be viewed from many, many different angles. It is very rare or almost impossible that an event can be negative from all points of view. Therefore, it is useful when something happens to try to look at it from different angles and then you can see the positive or beneficial aspects.

Moreover, if something happens, it is very useful immediately to make a comparison with some other event or with the events of other people or other nations. This is also very helpful in sustaining your peace of mind.

I will now explain, as a Buddhist monk, how to deal with death. Buddha taught the principles of the Four Noble Truths, the first of which is the Truth of Suffering. The Truth

Right, Woman beside new prayer flags just outside Lhasa, Tibet.

Below, Young Monks on the balcony of Tashikhyil Monastery.

210

of Suffering is taught within the context of three characteristics of existence, the first being impermanence. When talking about the nature of impermanence we must bear in mind that there are two levels. One is the coarse level, which is quite obvious and is the cessation of the continuation of a life or an event. But the impermanent nature which is being taught in relation to the Four Noble Truths refers to the more subtle aspect of impermanence, which is the transitory nature of existence.

66 **With the seed of the cause of events is the seed for their cessation and disintegration.** 99

Buddha's teaching of the more subtle aspects of the impermanent nature of existence aims at establishing an appreciation of the basic unsatisfactory nature of our existence. If you understand the nature of impermanence correctly, you will understand that it reveals that any existents which are causally produced, that is, which come about as a result of causes and conditions, entirely depend on causes and conditions for their existence.

Not only that, but the very causes and conditions which have produced them also bring about the disintegration and

cessation of those very entities. So, within the seed of the cause of events is the seed for their cessation and disintegration. When this is related to the understanding of the impermanent nature of our own aggregates, the body and mind, then here the cause refers to our own ignorant state of mind, which is the root of our existence, and this reveals that our very physical existence, our bodily existence, is very much governed by the force of an ignorant state of mind.

Right, His Holiness the Dalai Lama teaching at the Kalachakra Initiation, Spiti, India, August, 2000.

But it is by first reflecting upon the coarser levels of impermanence that one is eventually led to an appreciation of the subtle levels of impermanence. And by this, one will be able to confront and counteract grasping at permanence or eternal existence of one's own identity or self, because it is this grasping at permanence that forces us to cling onto this very "now-ness" or matters of one's lifetime alone. By releasing the grip of this grasping and enduring within us, we will be in a better position to appreciate the value of working for our future lifetimes.

66 **Buddhist practice greatly emphasizes the importance of the awareness of death and impermanence.** 99

One of the reasons why awareness of death and impermanence is so crucial in the Buddhist religious practice is that it
is considered that your state of mind at the time of death has
a very great effect on determining what form of rebirth you
might take. Whether it is a positive state of mind or a negative one will have a great effect. Therefore, Buddhist religious
practice greatly emphasizes the importance of the awareness
of death and impermanence.

Although the main purpose of a high degree of awareness
of impermanence is to train oneself so that at the time of
death one will be in a virtuous and positive state of mind,
and will be assured of a positive rebirth, there are other
benefits. One of the positive side-effects of maintaining a
very high degree of awareness of death is that it will prepare the individual to such an extent that, when the individual actually faces death, he or she will be in a better
position to maintain his or her presence of mind. Especially
in Tantric Buddhism, it is considered that the state of mind
which one experiences at the point of death is extremely
subtle and, because of the subtlety of the level of that consciousness, it also has a great power and impact upon one's
mental continuum. So in Tantric practices we find a lot of
emphasis placed on death-related meditations and also
reflections upon the process of death, so that the individual at the time of death not only retains his or her presence

of mind, but also is in a position to utilize that subtle state of consciousness effectively toward the realization of the path.

It is because of this that we find many Tantric meditations, technically known as the "deity yoga meditations" because they are meditations on deities, involve the dissolution process, reflecting upon the dissolution of elements which the individual experiences at the point of death. In fact, from the Tantric perspective, the entire process of existence is explained in terms of the three stages known as "death," "the intermediate state," and "rebirth." All of these three stages of existence are seen as states or manifestations of the consciousness and the energies that accompany or propel the consciousness, so that the intermediate state and rebirth are nothing other than various levels of the subtle consciousness and energy. An example of such fluctuating states can be found in our daily existence, when during the 24-hour day we go through a cycle of deep sleep, the waking period and the dream state. Our daily existence is in fact characterized by these three stages.

When talking about the distinctions that are made in the Tantric literature between the subtle and gross levels of consciousness and mind, I think it is important to bear in mind what exactly we mean by "mental consciousness." Often people get the impression that when we talk about the sixth mental consciousness there is some kind of autonomous type of consciousness which is totally independent from the bodily states and which is, in a way, the equivalent of the soul. But

Right, A young monk leading an old monk on horse-back near Phuhktal Monastery, Zanskar, India.

218

this is a misunderstanding. I personally think that if we were to examine our mental world we would find that most of our mental states and mental functions have direct physical correlates. Not only the sensory consciousness, but also much of what we would call mental consciousness has physiological bases and is intimately linked with the bodily states, just as scientists would say that the

brain and nervous system are the primary physiological bases of much of our conscious experience. Therefore, when the bodily states cease, these mental functions also cease.

But the question really is: what makes it possible for certain physical substances or physiological states to give rise to a mental event or a state of awareness? The Buddhist, particularly the Tantric, explanation points toward what is known as the subtle Clear Light state, which can be seen as independent from a physiological base. And it is this Clear Light state of mind which is the most subtle level of consciousness which, when it interacts with the physiological base, gives rise to all our conscious and cognitive events.

There are certain indications of the existence of what we call the Clear Light state of mind. There are incidents which generally tend to be more possible for religious practitioners.

Above, A monk making a ritual hand gesture (mudra) with his prayer beads, representing the ultimate offering of the universe as a mandala, Dharamsala, India.

For instance, among the Tibetan community in exile there have been cases where people have been pronounced clinically dead, that is, their brain function has ceased and the brain is dead but the decomposition of the body has not begun, and they remain in that state for days on end. For instance, my own late tutor, Kyabje Ling Rinpoche, remained in that state for 13 days. He was pronounced clinically dead and he had already experienced the death of the brain, but his body remained fresh and did not decompose for 13 days.

Now there must be some explanation for this. The Buddhist explanation is that, during that state, the individual is not actually dead but rather in the process of dying. Buddhists would explain that although the mind–body relationship may have ceased at the grosser, coarse level, it has not ceased at the subtle level. According to particular Tantric literature known as the Guhyasamaja Tantra, when an individual goes through the process of death, there is a certain process of dissolution. From that dissolution into the Clear Light state there is a reversal cycle and when that cycle reaches a certain stage, a new life begins that is called the rebirth. Then that rebirth remains and the individual again goes through a process of dissolution. In a way, death is at the intervening stage when the elements dissolve into the Clear Light and from there re-arise in another form. So death is nothing other than these intervening points when the individual's various physiological elements dissolve into the Clear Light point.

As regards the actual dissolution process of the various elements, the literature mentions different stages of dissolution and their accompanying signs. For instance, in the case of the dissolution of the coarser levels of elements, there are both internal and external signs and indications that mark the dissolution. When it comes to the subtle elements, there are only internal signs such as visions and so forth. There has been a growing interest among scientists who are doing research on death in these descriptions of the dissolution processes, particularly the internal and external signs. As a Buddhist, I think it is very important for us to be aware of the scientific investigations that are being undertaken. However, we must be able to distinguish between phenomena which still remain beyond the verification of existing scientific methodology and phenomena which can be seen as being disproved by existing scientific methods and investigation. I would say that if certain phenomena can be seen as being disproved by science, through scientific investigation and scientific methods, I think as Buddhists we will have to respect those conclusions.

As death becomes something familiar to you, as you have some knowledge of its processes and can recognize its external and internal indications, you are prepared for it. According to my own experience, I still have no confidence that at the moment of death I will really implement all these practices for which I have prepared. I have no guarantee! However, sometimes when I think about death I get some kind of excitement. Instead of fear, I have a feeling of curiosity and this makes it much easier for me to accept death. I wonder to what extent I can implement these practices. Of course, my only burden if I die today is, "Oh, what will happen to Tibet? What about Tibetan culture? What about the six million Tibetan people's rights?" This is my main concern. Otherwise, I feel almost no fear of death. Perhaps I have some kind of blind confidence! So it is good to reduce the fear of death. In my daily practice of prayer I visualize eight different deity yogas and eight different deaths. Perhaps when death comes all my preparation may fail. I hope not!

Right, A sacred masked dance at the Monlam Prayer Festival, Tashikhyil Monastery, Amdo, Eastern Tibet.

> **❝ Sometimes when I think about death I have a feeling of curiousity and this makes it much easier for me to accept death. ❞**

Anyway, I think that way is mentally very helpful in dealing with death. Even if there is no next life, there is some benefit if it relieves fear. And because there is less fear, one can be more fully prepared. Just as for battle, without preparation there is a good chance you will lose, but if you are fully prepared, there is more chance of defense. If you are fully

prepared then, at the moment of death, you can retain your peace of mind. It is peace of mind at the time of death which is the foundation for cultivating the proper motivation and that is the immediate guarantee of a good rebirth, of a better life to come. Particularly for the practitioner of the Maha-anuttarayoga Tantrayana, death is one of the rare opportunities to transform the subtle mind into wisdom.

As to what is in store for us after death, Buddhists talk about three realms of existence, technically known as "the form realm," "the formless realm," and "the desire realm." Both the form realm and the desire realm have an intervening stage before you take rebirth, known as "the intermediate state." What all of this points toward is that although the occasion of death provides us with the best opportunity to utilize our most subtle level of consciousness, transforming it into a path of wisdom, even if we are not able to seize that opportunity effectively, there is an intermediate state which, though grosser than at the time of death, is a lot more subtle than the consciousness at the time of rebirth. So there is another opportunity. And even if we are unable to seize this opportunity, there is rebirth and a continuing cycle.

So in order to seize the wonderful opportunity accorded at the time of death and, after that, during the intermediate state, we need first to train ourselves to be able to utilize those moments. For that, Buddhism teaches various

Left, A young monk beside a door of the main prayer hall of Tashikhyil Monastery, Amdo, Eastern Tibet.

techniques to enable the individual to apply certain meditative techniques during each of the dream, deep sleep, and waking states.

In conclusion, I think at the time of death a peaceful mind is essential no matter what you believe in, whether it is Buddhism or some other religion. At the moment of death, the individual should not seek to develop anger, hatred, and so on. That is very important at the conventional level. I think even non-believers see that it is better to pass away in a peaceful manner. It is much happier. Also, for those who believe in heaven or some other concept, it is also best to pass away peacefully with the thought of one's own God or belief in higher forces. For Buddhists and also other ancient Indian traditions which accept the rebirth or karma theory, naturally at the time of death a virtuous state of mind is beneficial.

Right, Young monks exchanging conversation during a ceremony at Tashikhyil Monastery, Amdo, Eastern Tibet.

DEALING WITH ANGER AND EMOTION

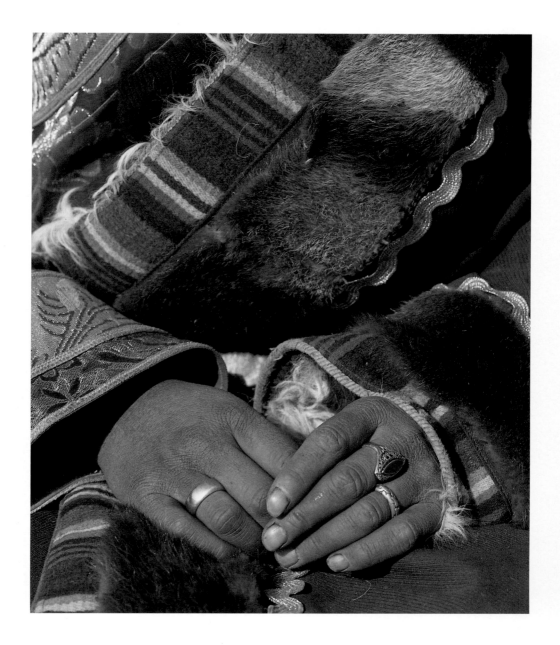

> **" According to my experience, it is clear that if each individual makes an effort then he or she can change. "**

Anger and hatred are two of our closest friends. When I was young I had quite a close relationship with anger. Then eventually I found a lot of disagreement with anger. By using common sense, with the help of compassion and wisdom, I now have a more powerful argument with which to defeat anger.

According to my experience, it is clear that if each individual makes an effort then he or she can change. Of course, change is not immediate and it takes a lot of time. In order to change and deal with emotions it is crucial to analyze which thoughts are useful, constructive, and of benefit to us. I mean mainly those thoughts which make us calmer, more relaxed, and which give us peace of mind, versus those thoughts which create uneasiness, fear, and frustration. This analysis is similar to one which we might use for external things, such as plants. Some plants, flowers, and fruit are good for us, so we use them and grow them. Those plants which are poisonous or harmful to us, we learn to recognize and even sometimes to destroy.

Left, A detailed close-up of the hands of a pilgrim woman wearing a fine chuba at Tashikhyil Monastery, Amdo, Eastern Tibet.

There is a similarity with the inner world. It is too simplistic to speak about the "body" and the "mind." Within the body there are billions of different particles. Similarly, there are many different thoughts and a variety of states of mind. It is wise to take a close look into the world of your mind and to make the distinction between beneficial and harmful states of mind. Once you can recognize the value of good states of mind, you can increase or foster them.

Buddha taught the principles of the Four Noble Truths and these form the foundation of the Buddha Dharma. The Third Noble Truth is cessation. According to Nagarjuna, in this context cessation means the state of mind or mental quality which, through practice and effort, ceases all the negative emotions. Nagarjuna defines true cessation as a state in which the individual has reached a perfected state of mind which is free from the effects of various afflictive and negative emotions and thoughts. Such a state of true cessation is, according to Buddhism, a genuine Dharma and therefore is the refuge that all practising Buddhists seek. Buddha becomes an object of refuge, worthy of respect, because Buddha has realized that state. Therefore one's reverence to the Buddha, and the reason one seeks refuge in the Buddha, is not because Buddha was from the beginning a special person, but because Buddha realized the state of true cessation. Similarly, the spiritual community, or sangha, is taken as an object of refuge because the members of the spiritual

Right, Monks in full ceremonial attire walking to an early morning prayer ceremony, Tashikhyil Monastery.

community are individuals who are either already on, or are embarking on, the path leading to that state of cessation.

We find that the true state of cessation can be understood only in terms of a state of mind which is free from, or which has been purified of, negative emotions and thoughts due to the application of antidotes and counter-forces. True cessation is a state of mind and the factors that lead to this are also functions of the mind. Also, the basis on which the purification takes place is the mental continuum. Therefore, an understanding of the nature of the mind is crucial for Buddhist practice. By saying this, I do not mean that everything which exists is simply a reflection or projection of the mind and that apart from the mind nothing exists. But because of the importance of understanding the nature of mind in Buddhist practice, people often describe Buddhism as "a science of the mind."

Generally speaking, in Buddhist literature, a negative emotion or thought is defined as "a state which causes disturbance within one's mind." These afflictive emotions and thoughts are factors that create unhappiness and turmoil within us. Emotion in general is not necessarily something negative. At a scientific conference which I attended along with many psychologists and neuro-scientists, it was concluded that even Buddhas have emotion, according to the definition of emotion found in various scientific disciplines. So karuna (infinite compassion or kindness) can be described as a kind of emotion.

Naturally, emotions can be positive and negative. However, when talking about anger, etc., we are dealing with negative emotions. Negative emotions are those which immediately create some kind of unhappiness or uneasiness and which, in the long run, create certain actions. Those actions ultimately lead to harm to others, and this brings pain or suffering to oneself. This is what we mean by negative emotions.

Right, A young monk in ceremonial costume participating in a sacred dance, Tashikhyil Monastery, Amdo, Eastern Tibet.

66 There are meditative techniques which enable the transformation of the energy of anger. 99

One negative emotion is anger. Perhaps there are two types of anger. One type of anger could be transformed into a positive emotion. For example, if one has a sincere compassionate motivation and concern for someone, and that person

238

does not heed one's warning about his or her actions, then there is no other alternative except the use of some kind of force to stop that person's misdeeds. In Tantrayana practice there are meditative techniques which enable the transformation of the energy of anger. This is the reason behind the wrathful deities. On the basis of compassionate motivation, anger may in some cases be useful because it gives us extra energy and enables us to act swiftly.

However, anger usually leads to hatred and hatred is always negative. Hatred harbours ill will. I usually analyze anger on two levels: on the basic human level and on the Buddhist level. From the human level, without any reference to a religious tradition or ideology, we can look at the sources of our happiness: good health, material facilities, and good companions. Now from the standpoint of health, negative emotions such as hatred are very bad. Since people generally try to take care of their health, one technique people can use is their mental attitude. Your mental state should always remain calm. Even if some anxiety occurs, as it is bound to in life, you should always be calm. Like a wave which rises from the water and dissolves back into the water, these disturbances are very short, so they should not affect your basic mental attitude. Though you cannot eliminate all negative emotions, if your basic mental attitude is healthy and calm, it will not be much affected. If you remain calm, your blood pressure and so on remains more normal and as a result your

Left, A chorten (reliquary) in a field after a fresh snow fall, near Lhasa, Tibet.

health will improve. While I cannot say scientifically why this is so, I believe that my own physical condition is improving as I get older. I have had the same medicine, the same doctor, the same food, so it must be due to my mental state. Some people say to me, "You must have some kind of special Tibetan medicine." But I don't!

As I mentioned earlier, when I was young I was quite short-tempered. I would sometimes excuse this by saying that it was because my father was short-tempered, as if it was something genetic. But as time passes, I think that now I have almost no hatred toward anybody, including toward those Chinese who are creating misery and suffering for Tibetans. Even toward them, I really do not feel any kind of hatred.

Some of my close friends have high blood pressure, yet they never come near to having crises in their health and they never feel tired. Over the years I have met some very good practitioners. Meanwhile, there are other friends who have great material comfort yet, when we start to talk, after the initial few nice words, they begin to complain and grieve. In spite of their material prosperity, these people do not have calm or peaceful minds. As a result, they are always worrying about their digestion, their sleep, everything! Therefore it is clear that mental calmness is a very important factor for good health. If you want good health, don't ask a doctor, look within yourself. Try to utilize some of your potential. This even costs less!

Right, Pilgrims performing a "kora" or circumambulation of a large chorten (reliquary), Tashikhyil Monastery, Amdo, Eastern Tibet.

The second source of happiness is material facilities. Sometimes when I wake up in the early morning, if my mood is not very good, then when I look at my watch I feel uncomfortable because of my mood. Then on other days, due perhaps to the previous day's experience, when I wake up my mood is pleasant and peaceful. At that time, when I look at my watch I see it as extraordinarily beautiful. Yet it is the same watch, isn't it? The difference comes from my mental attitude. Whether our use of our material facilities provides genuine satisfaction or not depends on our mental attitude.

❝ It is obvious that when you are mentally calm you are honest and open-minded. ❞

It is bad for our material facilities if our mind is dominated by anger. To speak again from my own experience, when I was young I sometimes repaired watches. I tried and failed many times. Sometimes I would lose my patience and hit the watch! During those moments, my anger altered my whole attitude and afterwards I felt very sorry for my actions. If my goal was to repair the watch, then why did I hit it on the table? Again you can see how one's mental attitude is

Right, A monk playing a short ritual horn in a ceremony at the Jokhang Temple, Lhasa, Tibet. This instrument is modelled upon the form of a human thighbone trumpet.

Left, A monk
walking down a
snowy path towards
Tashikhyil Monastery,
Amdo, Eastern Tibet.

crucial in order to utilize material facilities for one's genuine satisfaction or benefit.

The third source of happiness is our companions. It is obvious that when you are mentally calm you are honest and open-minded. I will give you an example. Perhaps 14 or 15 years ago, there was an Englishman named Phillips who had a close relationship with the Chinese government, including Chou En Lai and other leaders. He had known them for many years and he was close friends with the Chinese. One time, in 1977 or 1978, Phillips came to Dharamsala to see me. He brought some films with him and he told me about all the good aspects of China. At the beginning of our meeting there was a big disagreement between us, for we held completely different opinions. In his view, the presence of the Chinese in Tibet was something good. In my opinion, and according to many reports, the situation was not good. As usual, I had no particular negative feeling toward him. I just felt that he held these views due to ignorance. With openness, I continued our conversation. I argued that those Tibetans who had joined the Chinese Communist Party as early as 1930 and who had participated in the Sino–Japanese War and had welcomed the Chinese invasion and enthusiastically collaborated with the Chinese Communists did so because they believed that it was a golden opportunity to develop Tibet, from the viewpoint of Marxist ideology. These people had collaborated with the Chinese out of genuine hope. Then, around 1956 or 1957, most of them were dismissed from the various Chinese offices, some were imprisoned, and others disappeared. Thus I explained that we are not anti-Chinese or anti-Communist. In fact, I sometimes think of myself as a half-Marxist, half-Buddhist. I explained all these different things to him with sincere motivation and openness and after some time his attitude completely changed. This instance gives me some confirmation that even if there is a big difference of opinion, you can communicate on a human level. You can put aside these different opinions and communicate as human beings. I think that is one way to create positive feelings in other people's minds.

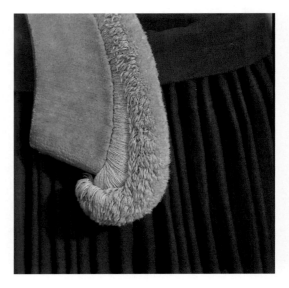

Above A detail of a monk's robe and ceremonial hat, Tashikhyil Monastery.

Also, I am quite sure that if this Fourteenth Dalai Lama smiled less, perhaps I would have fewer friends in various places. My attitude toward other people is to always look at them from the human level. On that level, whether president, queen or beggar, there is no difference, provided that there is genuine human feeling with a genuine human smile of affection.

I think that there is more value in genuine human feeling than in status and so on. I am just a simple human being.

Through my experience and mental discipline, a certain new attitude has developed. This is nothing special. You, who I think have had a better education and more experience than myself, have more potential to change within yourself. I come from a small village with no modern education and no deep awareness of the world. Also, from the age of 15 or 16 I had an unthinkable sort of burden. Therefore each of you should feel that you have great potential and that, with self-confidence and a little more effort, change really is possible if you want it. If you feel that your present way of life is unpleasant or has some difficulties, then don't look at these negative things. See the positive side, the potential, and make an effort. I think that there is already at that point some kind of partial guarantee of success. If we utilize all our positive human energy or human qualities we can overcome these human problems.

So, as far as our contact with fellow human beings is concerned, our mental attitude is very crucial. Even for a nonbeliever, just a simple honest human being, the ultimate source of happiness is in our mental attitude. Even if you have good health, material facilities used in the proper way, and good relations with other human beings, the main cause of a happy life is within. If you have more money you sometimes have more worries and you still feel hungry for more. Ultimately you become a slave of money. While money is very useful and necessary, it is not the ultimate

source of happiness. Similarly, education, if not well balanced, can sometimes create more trouble, more anxiety, more greed, more desire, and more ambition – in short, more mental suffering. Friends, too, are sometimes very troublesome.

Now you can see how to minimize anger and hatred. First, it is extremely important to realize the negativity of these emotions in general, particularly hatred. I consider hatred to be the ultimate enemy. By "enemy" I mean the person or factor which directly or indirectly destroys our interest. Our interest is that which ultimately creates happiness.

We can also speak of the external enemy. For example, in my own case, our Chinese brothers and sisters are destroying Tibetan rights and, in that way, more suffering and anxiety develop. But no matter how forceful this is, it cannot destroy the supreme source of my happiness, which is my calmness of mind. This is something an external enemy cannot destroy. Our country can be invaded, our possessions can be destroyed, our friends can be killed, but these are secondary for our mental happiness. The ultimate source of my mental happiness is my peace of mind. Nothing can destroy this except my own anger.

Left, The ornately decorated doors of a prayer hall in Tashikhyil Monastery, Amdo, Eastern Tibet.

66 **Once you try to control or discipline your anger, then eventually even big events will not cause anger.** 99

Moreover, you can escape or hide from an external enemy and sometimes you can even cheat the enemy. For example, if there is someone who disturbs my peace of mind, I can escape by locking my door and sitting quietly alone. But I cannot do that with anger! Wherever I go, it is always there. Even though I have locked my room, the anger is still inside. Unless you adopt a certain method, there is no possibility of escape. Therefore, hatred or anger – and here I mean negative anger – is ultimately the real destroyer of my peace of mind and is therefore my true enemy.

Some people believe that to suppress emotion is not good, that it is much better to let it out. I think there are differences between various negative emotions. For example, with frustration, there is a certain frustration which develops as a result of past events. Sometimes if you hide these negative events, such as sexual abuse, then consciously or unconsciously this creates problems. Therefore, in this case, it is much better to express the frustration and let it out. However, according to our experience with anger, if you do not make an attempt to reduce it, it will remain with you and even increase. Then even with small incidents you will immediately get angry. Once you try to control or discipline your anger, then eventually even big events will not cause anger. Through training and discipline you can change.

When anger comes, there is one important technique to help you keep your peace of mind. You should not become

Right, Monks seated in meditation on the steps of Tashikhyil Monastery, Amdo, Eastern Tibet.

dissatisfied or frustrated, because this is the cause of anger and hatred. There is a natural connection between cause and effect. Once certain causes and conditions are fully met, it is extremely difficult to prevent that causal process from coming to fruition. It is crucial to examine the situation so that at a very early stage one is able to put a stop to the causal process. Then it does not continue to an advanced stage. In the Buddhist text *A Guide to the Bodhisattva Way of Life*, the great scholar Shantideva mentions that it is very important to ensure that a person does not get into a situation which leads to dissatisfaction, because dissatisfaction is the seed of anger. This means that one must adopt a certain outlook toward one's material possessions, toward one's companions and friends, and toward various situations.

Left, The Potala
Palace, the
traditional historical
abode of His Holiness
the Dalai Lama
at dawn in Lhasa,
Tibet.

❝ By bringing about a change in our outlook toward things and events, all phenomena can become sources of happiness. ❞

Our feelings of dissatisfaction, unhappiness, loss of hope, and so forth are in fact related to all phenomena. If we do not adopt the right outlook, it is possible that anything and everything could cause us frustration. For some people

Left, The "Emblem of the Three Great Bodhisattvas" with the sword representing Manjushri's widsom, the parrot Vajrapani's power and the duck Avalokiteshvara's compassion, Tashikhyil Monastery.

even the name of the Buddha could conceivably cause anger and frustration, although it may not be the case when someone has a direct personal encounter with a Buddha. Therefore, all phenomena have the potential to create frustration and dissatisfaction in us. Yet phenomena are part of reality and we are subject to the laws of existence. So this leaves us only one option: to change our own attitude. By bringing about a change in our outlook toward things and events, all phenomena can become friends or sources of happiness, instead of becoming enemies or sources of frustration.

A particular case is that of an enemy. Of course, in one way, having an enemy is very bad. It disturbs our mental peace and destroys some of our good things. But if we look at it from another angle, only an enemy gives us the opportunity to practice patience. No one else provides us with the opportunity for tolerance. For example, as a Buddhist, I think Buddha completely failed to provide us with the opportunity to practice tolerance and patience. Some members of the sangha may provide us with this, but otherwise it is quite rare. Since we do not know the majority of the five billion human beings on this earth, therefore the majority of people do not give us an opportunity to show tolerance or patience either. Only those people whom we know and who create problems for us really provide us with a good opportunity to practice tolerance and patience.

Seen from this angle, the enemy is the greatest teacher for our practice. Shantideva argues very brilliantly that enemies, or the perpetrators of harm upon us, are in fact objects worthy of respect and are worthy of being regarded as our precious teachers. One might object that our enemies cannot be considered worthy of our respect because they have no intention of helping us; the fact that they are helpful and beneficial to us is merely a coincidence. Shantideva says that if this is the case then why should we, as practicing Buddhists, regard the state of cessation as an object worthy of refuge when cessation is a mere state of mind and on its part has no intention of helping us. One may then say that although this is true, at least with cessation there is no intention of harming us, whereas enemies, contrary to having the intention of helping us, in fact intend to harm us. Therefore an enemy is not an object worthy of respect. Shantideva says that it is this very intention of harming us which makes the enemy very special. If the enemy had no intention of harming us, then we would not classify that person as an enemy, therefore our attitude would be completely different. It is his or her very intention of harming us which makes that person an enemy, and because of that the enemy provides us with an opportunity to practice tolerance and patience. Therefore an enemy is indeed a precious teacher. By thinking along these lines you can eventually reduce the negative mental emotions, particularly hatred.

Right, A monk wearing the brocade robes, bone ornaments and skull crown of a tantric deity while performing a sacred dance at Sertang Monastery.

Sometimes people feel that anger is useful because it brings extra energy and boldness. When we encounter difficulties, we may see anger as a protector. But though anger brings us more energy, that energy is essentially a blind one. There is no guarantee that that anger and energy will not become destructive to our own interests. Therefore hatred and anger are not at all useful.

> **One can overcome the forces of negative emotions, like anger and hatred, by cultivating their counter-forces, like love and compassion.**

Another question is that if you always remain humble then others may take advantage of you and how should you react? It is quite simple: you should act with wisdom or common sense, without anger and hatred. If the situation is such that you need some sort of action on your part, you can, without anger, take a counter-measure. In fact, such actions which follow true wisdom rather than anger are in reality more effective. A counter-measure taken in the midst of anger may often go wrong. In a very competitive society, it is sometimes necessary to take a counter-measure. We can again examine

Above, "Mani" stones (stones with prayers and symbols inscribed on them) beside a chorten (reliquary) on the route to Phuktal Monastery in Zanskar, India.

the Tibetan situation. As I mentioned earlier, we are following a genuinely non-violent and compassionate way, but this does not mean that we should just bow down to the aggressors' action and give in. Without anger and without hatred, we can manage more effectively.

There is another type of practice of tolerance which involves consciously taking on the sufferings of others. I am thinking of situations in which, by engaging in certain activities, we are aware of the hardships, difficulties, and problems that are involved in the short term, but are convinced that such actions will have a very beneficial long-term effect. Because of our attitude, and our commitment and wish to bring about that long-term benefit, we sometimes consciously and deliberately take upon ourselves the hardships and problems that are involved in the short term.

One of the effective means by which one can overcome the forces of negative emotions like anger and hatred is by cultivating their counter-forces, such as the positive qualities of mind like love and compassion.

GIVING AND RECEIVING

Left, Chorten and prayer flags at dawn on the Kunzum La pass between the Spiti valley and Lahaul, Himachal Pradesh, India.

Compassion is the most wonderful and precious thing. When we talk about compassion, it is encouraging to note that basic human nature is, I believe, compassionate and gentle. Sometimes I argue with friends who believe that human nature is more negative and aggressive. I argue that if you study the structure of the human body you will see that it is akin to those species of mammals whose way of life is more gentle or peaceful. Sometimes I half joke that our hands are arranged in such a manner that they are good for hugging, rather than hitting. If our hands were mainly meant for hitting, then these beautiful fingers would not be necessary. For example, if the fingers remain extended, boxers cannot hit forcefully, so they have to make fists. So I think that means that our basic physical structure creates a compassionate or gentle kind of nature.

If we look at relationships, marriage and conception are very important. As I said earlier, marriage should not be based on blind love or an extreme sort of mad love; it should be based on a knowledge of one another and an understanding that you are suitable to live together. Marriage is not for temporary satisfaction, but for some kind of sense of responsibility. That is the genuine love which is the basis of marriage.

The proper conception of a child takes place in that kind of moral or mental attitude. While the child is in the mother's womb, the mother's calmness of mind has a very positive effect on the unborn child, according to some scientists. If the mother's mental state is negative, for instance if she is frustrated or angry, then it is very harmful to the healthy development of the unborn child. One scientist has told me that the first few weeks after birth is the most important period, for during that time the child's brain is growing. During that period, the mother's touch or that of someone who is acting like a mother is crucial. This shows that even though the child may not realize who is who, it somehow physically needs someone else's affection. Without that, it is very damaging for the healthy development of the brain.

66 **Lessons we learn from teachers who are not just good, but who also show affection for the student, go deep into our minds.** 99

After birth, the first act by the mother is to give the child nourishing milk. If the mother lacks affection or kind feelings for the child, then the milk will not flow. If the mother feeds her baby with gentle feelings toward the child, in spite of her own illness or pain, as a result the milk flows

freely. This kind of attitude is like a precious jewel. Moreover, from the other side, if the child lacks some kind of close feeling toward the mother, it may not suckle. This shows how wonderful the act of affection from both sides is. That is the beginning of our lives.

Similarly with education, it is my experience that those lessons which we learn from teachers who are not just good, but who also show affection for the student, go deep into our minds. Lessons from other sorts of teachers may not. Although you may be compelled to study and may fear the teacher, the lessons may not sink in. Much depends on the affection from the teacher.

Likewise, when we go to a hospital, irrespective of the doctor's quality, if the doctor shows genuine feeling and deep concern for us, and if he or she smiles, then we feel OK. But if the doctor shows little human affection, then even though he or she may be a very great expert, we may feel unsure and nervous. This is human nature.

Lastly, we can reflect on our lives. When we are young and again when we are old, we depend heavily on the affection of others. Between these stages we usually feel that we can do everything without help from others and that other people's affection is simply not important. But at this stage I think it is very important to keep deep human affection. When people in a big town or city feel lonely, this does not mean that they lack human companions, but

rather that they lack human affection. As a result of this, their mental health eventually becomes very poor. On the other hand, those people who grow up in an atmosphere of human affection have a much more positive and gentle development of their bodies, their minds, and their behavior. Children who have grown up lacking that atmosphere usually have more negative attitudes. This very clearly shows the basic human nature. Also, as I have mentioned, the human body appreciates peace of mind. Things that are disturbing to us have a very bad effect upon our health. This shows that the whole structure of our health is such that it is suited to an atmosphere of human affection. Therefore, our potential for compassion is there. The only issue is whether or not we realize this and utilize it.

The basic aim of my explanation is to show that by nature we are compassionate, that compassion is something very necessary, and something which we can develop. It is important to know the exact meaning of compassion. Different philosophies and traditions have different interpretations of the meaning of love and compassion. Some of my Christian friends believe that love cannot develop without God's grace; in other words, to develop love and compassion you need faith. The Buddhist interpretation is that genuine compassion is based on a clear acceptance or recognition that others, like oneself, want happiness

Left, Monks waiting for dawn to unfurl a giant thangkha at Sertang Monastery, Tagtsang Lhamo, Amdo, Eastern Tibet on the 13th day of the Monlam prayer festival.

and have the right to overcome suffering. On that basis one develops some kind of concern about the welfare of others, irrespective of one's attitude to oneself. That is compassion.

> **❝ All sentient beings should be looked on as equal. You can then gradually develop genuine compassion for all of them. ❞**

Your love and compassion toward your friends is in many cases actually attachment. This feeling is not based on the realization that all beings have an equal right to be happy and to overcome suffering. Instead, it is based on the idea that something is "mine," "my friend," or something good for "me." That is attachment. Thus, when that person's attitude toward you changes, your feeling of closeness immediately disappears. With the other way, you develop some kind of concern irrespective of the other person's attitude to you, simply because that person is a fellow human being and has every right to overcome suffering. Whether that person remains neutral to you or even becomes your enemy, your concern should remain because of his or her right. That is the main difference. Genuine compassion is much healthier; it is unbiased, and it is

Right, Monks and pilgrims gather around a giant thangkha in a ceremony at Sertang Monastery.

Left, Monks in front of a giant thangkha in a ceremony at Sertang Monastery.

based on reason. By contrast, attachment is narrow-minded and biased.

Actually, genuine compassion and attachment are contradictory. According to Buddhist practice, to develop genuine compassion you must first practice the meditation of equalization and equanimity, detaching oneself from those people who are very close to you. Then, you must remove negative feelings toward your enemies. All sentient beings should be looked on as equal. On that basis, you can gradually develop genuine compassion for all of them. It must be said that genuine compassion is not like pity or a feeling that others are somehow lower than yourself. Rather, with genuine compassion you view others as more important than yourself.

As I pointed out earlier, in order to generate genuine compassion, first of all one must go through the training of equanimity. This becomes very important, because without a sense of equanimity toward all, one's feelings toward others will be biased. So now I will give you a brief example of a Buddhist meditative training on developing equanimity. First, you should think about a small group of people whom you know, such as your friends and relatives, toward whom you have attachment. Second, you should think about some people to whom you feel totally indifferent. And third, think about some people whom you dislike. Once you have imagined these different people, you should try to let your mind go into its natural state and see how it would normally respond to an encounter with these people. You will notice that your natural reaction would be that of attachment toward your friends, that of dislike toward the people whom you consider enemies, and that of total indifference toward those whom you consider neutral. Then you should try to question yourself.

Above, Monks holding a parasol, victory banners and ritual hand drums.

You should compare the effects of the two opposing attitudes you have toward your friends and your enemies, and see why you should have such fluctuating states of mind toward these two different groups of people. You should see what effects such reactions have on your mind and try to see the futility of relating to them in such an extreme manner. I have already discussed the pros and cons of harboring hatred and generating anger toward enemies, and I have also spoken a little about the defects of being extremely attached toward friends and so on. You should reflect upon this and then try to minimize your strong emotions toward these two opposing groups of people. Then, most importantly, you should reflect on the fundamental equality between yourself and all other sentient beings. Just as you have the instinctive natural desire to be happy and overcome suffering, so do all sentient beings; just as you have the right to fulfil this innate aspiration, so do all sentient beings. So on what exact grounds do you discriminate?

If we look at humanity as a whole, we are social animals. Moreover, the structures of the modern economy, education, and so on, illustrate that the world has become a smaller place and that we depend heavily on one another. Under such circumstances, I think the only option is to live and work together harmoniously, and keep in our minds the interest of the whole of humanity. That is the only outlook and way we must adopt for our survival.

" The only option is to live and work together harmoniously, and keep in our minds the interest of the whole of humanity. "

By nature, especially as a human being, my interests are not independent of others. My happiness depends on others' happiness. So when I see happy people, automatically I also feel a little bit happier than when I see people in a difficult situation. For example, when we see pictures on television which show people starving in Somalia,

Left, A wall
painting of White
Manjughosha
(Manjushri), the
bodhisattva of
wisdom, Tashikhyil
Monastery.

including old people and young children, then we automatically feel sad, regardless of whether that sadness can lead to some kind of active help or not.

Moreover, in our daily lives we are now utilizing many good facilities, including things like air-conditioned houses. All these things or facilities became possible, not because of ourselves, but because of many other people's direct or indirect involvement. Everything comes together. It is impossible to return to the way of life of a few centuries ago, when we depended on simple instruments, not all these machines. It is very clear to us that the facilities that we are enjoying now are the products of the activities of many people. In 24 hours you sleep on a bed – many people have been involved in that – and in the preparation of your food, too, especially for the non-vegetarian. Fame is definitely a product of other people – without the presence of other people the concept of fame would not even make sense. Also, the interest of Europe depends on America's interest and Western Europe's interest depends on the Eastern European economic situation. Each continent is heavily dependent on the others; that is the reality. Thus many of the things that we desire, such as wealth, fame and so forth, could not come into being without the active or indirect participation and co-operation of many other people.

Therefore, since we all have an equal right to be happy and since we are all linked to one another, no matter how important an individual is, logically the interest of the other five billion people on the planet is more important than that of one single person. By thinking along these lines, you can eventually develop a sense of global responsibility. Modern environmental problems, such as the depletion of the ozone layer, also clearly show us the need for world co-operation. It seems that with development, the whole world has become much smaller, but the human consciousness is still lagging behind.

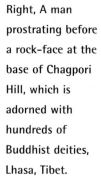

> 66 **If any individual is compassionate and altruistic, wherever that person moves, he or she will immediately make friends.** 99

This is not a question of religious practice, but a question of the future of humanity. This kind of wider or more altruistic attitude is very relevant in today's world. If we look at the situation from various angles, such as the complexity and inter-connectedness of the nature of modern existence, then we will gradually notice a change in our outlook, so that when we say "others" and when we think of others, we will no longer dismiss them as irrelevant to us. We will no longer feel indifferent.

Right, A man prostrating before a rock-face at the base of Chagpori Hill, which is adorned with hundreds of Buddhist deities, Lhasa, Tibet.

Left, A Monk
walking along the
roof of Sakya
Monastery, Tibet.

If you think only of yourself, if you forget the rights and well-being of others, or, worse still, if you exploit others, ultimately you will lose. You will have no friends who will show concern for your well-being. Moreover, if a tragedy befalls you, instead of feeling concerned, others might even secretly rejoice. By contrast, if an individual is compassionate and altruistic, and has the interests of others in mind, then irrespective of whether that person knows a lot of people, wherever that person moves, he or she will immediately make friends. And when that person faces a tragedy, there will be plenty of people who will come to help.

A true friendship develops on the basis of genuine human affection, not money or power. Of course, due to your power or wealth, more people may approach you with big smiles or gifts. But deep down these are not real friends of yours; these are friends of your wealth or power. As long as your fortune remains, then these people will often approach you. But when your fortunes decline, they will no longer be there. With this type of friend, nobody will make a sincere effort to help you if you need it. That is the reality.

Genuine human friendship is on the basis of human affection, irrespective of your position. Therefore, the more you show concern about the welfare and rights of others, the more you are a genuine friend. The more you remain open and sincere, then ultimately more benefits will come to you. If you forget or do not bother about others, then eventually you will lose your own benefit. So sometimes I tell people, if we really are selfish, then wise selfishness is much better than the selfishness of ignorance and narrow-mindedness.

For Buddhist practitioners, the development of wisdom is also very important – and here I mean wisdom which realizes Shunya, the ultimate nature of reality. The realization of Shunya gives you at least some kind of positive sense about cessation. Once you have some kind of feeling for the possibility of cessation, then it becomes clear that suffering is not final and that there is an alternative. If there is an alternative, then it is worth making an effort. If only two of the Buddha's Four Noble Truths exist – suffering and the cause of suffering -then there is not much meaning. But the other two Noble Truths, including cessation, point toward an alternative way of existence. There is a possibility of ending suffering. So it is worthwhile to realize the nature of suffering. Therefore wisdom is extremely important in increasing compassion infinitely.

So that is how one engages in the practice of Buddhism: there is an application of the faculty of wisdom, using intelligence, and an understanding of the nature of reality, together with the skilful means of generating compassion. I think that in your daily lives and in all sorts of your professional work, you can use this compassionate motivation.

Right, A senior monk holding a ritual vase containing the gathered sand from the Kalachakra Mandala, Ki Monastery, Spiti, India.

Left, Monks at dawn on the roof of Nechung Monastery.

Of course, in the field of education, there is no doubt that compassionate motivation is important and relevant. Irrespective of whether you are a believer or non-believer, compassion for the students' lives or futures, not only for their examinations, makes your work as a teacher much more effective. With that motivation, I think your students will remember you for the whole of their lives.

Similarly, in the field of health, there is an expression in Tibetan which says that the effectiveness of the treatment depends on how warm-hearted the physician is. Because of this expression, when treatments from a certain doctor do not work, people blame the doctor's character, speculating that perhaps that he or she was not a kind person. The poor doctor sometimes gets a very bad name! So in the medical field there is no doubt that compassionate motivation is something very relevant.

    Human compassion, or what I sometimes call 'human affection', is the key factor for all human business.

I think this is also the case with lawyers and politicians. If politicians and lawyers had more compassionate motivation then there would be less scandal. And as a result the whole community would get more peace. I think the work of politics would become more effective and more respected.

Finally, in my view, the worst thing is warfare. But even warfare with human affection and with human compassion is much less destructive. The completely mechanized warfare that is without human feeling is worse.

Also, I think compassion and a sense of responsibility can also enter into the fields of science and engineering. Of course, from a purely scientific point of view, awful weapons such as nuclear bombs are remarkable achievements. But we can say that these are negative because they bring immense suffering to the world. Therefore, if we do not take into account human pain, human feelings, and human compassion, there is no demarcation between right and wrong. Therefore, human compassion can reach everywhere.

I find it a little bit difficult to apply this principle of compassion to the field of economics. But economists are human beings and of course they also need human affection, without which they would suffer. However, if you think only of profit, irrespective of the consequences, then drug dealers are not wrong, because, from the economic viewpoint, they are also making tremendous profits. But because this is very harmful for society and for the community, we call this wrong and name these people

Right, Bundles of prayer flags and long rolls of printed mantras on sale at the Barkhor Market in front of the Jokhang Temple, Lhasa, Tibet.

Left, A monk performs a sacred dance, Tashikhyil Monastery.

criminals. If that is the case, then I think arms dealers are in the same category. The arms trade is equally dangerous and irresponsible.

So I think for these reasons, human compassion, or what I sometimes call "human affection," is the key factor for all human business. Just as you see that with the palm of our hand all five fingers become useful, if these fingers were not connected to the palm they would be useless. Similarly, every human action that is without human feeling becomes dangerous. With human feeling and an appreciation of human values, all human activities become constructive.

Even religion, which is supposedly good for humanity, can become foul without that basic human compassionate attitude. Unfortunately even now there are problems which are entirely down to different religions. So human compassion is something fundamental. If that is there, then all other human activities become more useful.

Generally speaking, I have the impression that in education and some other areas there is some neglect of the issue of human motivation. Perhaps in ancient times religion was supposed to carry this responsibility. But now in the community, religion generally seems a little bit old-fashioned, so people are losing interest in it and in deeper human values. However, I think these should be two separate things. If you have respect for or interest in religion, that is good. But even

if you have no interest in religion, you should not forget the importance of these deeper human values.

There are various positive side-effects of enhancing one's feeling of compassion. One of them is that the greater the force of your compassion, the greater your resilience in confronting hardships and your ability to transform them into more positive conditions. One form of practice that seems to be quite effective is found in *A Guide to the Bodhisattva Way of Life*, a classic Buddhist text. In this practice you visualize your old self, the embodiment of self-centerdness, selfishness and so on, and then visualize a group of people who represent the masses of other sentient beings. Then you adopt a third person's point of view as a neutral, unbiased observer and make a comparative assessment of the value, the interests, and then the importance of these two groups. Also try to reflect upon the faults of being totally oblivious to the well-being of other sentient beings and so on, and what this old self has really achieved as a result of leading such a way of life. Then reflect on the other sentient beings and see how important their well-being is, the need to serve them and so forth, and see what you, as a third neutral observer, would conclude as to whose interests and well-being are more important. You would naturally begin to feel more inclined toward the countless others.

I also think that the greater the force of your altruistic attitude toward sentient beings, the more courageous you

Left, His Holiness the Dalai Lama at the Kalachakra Initiation, Spiti, India, August 2000.

become. The greater your courage, the less you feel prone to discouragement and loss of hope. Therefore, compassion is also a source of inner strength. With increased inner strength it is possible to develop firm determination and with determination there is a greater chance of success, no matter what obstacles there may be. On the other hand, if you feel hesitation, fear, and a lack of self-confidence, then often you will develop a pessimistic attitude. I consider that to be the real seed of failure. With a pessimistic attitude you cannot accomplish even something you could easily achieve. Whereas even if something is difficult to achieve, if you have an unshakeable determination there is eventually the possibility of achievement. Therefore, even in the conventional sense, compassion is very important for a successful future.

Above, Freshly printed pages for prayer books, Ganden Monastery, Tibet.

66 Every religion teaches the same message: be a warm-hearted person. They all emphasize compassion and forgiveness. 99

As I pointed out earlier, depending on the level of your wisdom, there are different levels of compassion, such as compassion which is motivated by genuine insight into the ultimate nature of reality, compassion which is motivated by the appreciation of the impermanent nature of existence, and compassion which is motivated by awareness of the suffering of other sentient beings. The level of your wisdom, or the depth of your insight into the nature of reality, determines the level of compassion that you will experience. From the Buddhist viewpoint, compassion with wisdom is very essential. It is as if compassion is like a very honest person and wisdom is like a very able person – if you join these two, then the result is something very effective.

I see compassion, love, and forgiveness as common ground for all different religions, irrespective of tradition or philosophy. Although there are fundamental differences between different religious ideas, such as the acceptance of an Almighty Creator, every religion teaches us the same message: be a warm-hearted person. All of them emphasize the importance of compassion and forgiveness. Now in ancient times when the various religions were based in different places and there was less communication between them, there was no need for pluralism among the various religious traditions. But today, the world has become much smaller, so communication between different religious

Left, Samding monastery in the late afternoon light as seen from Nakartse, Tibet.

faiths has become very strong. Under such circumstances, I think pluralism among religious believers is very essential. Once you see the value to humanity through the centuries of these different religions through unbiased, objective study then there is plenty of reason to accept or to respect all these different religions. After all, in humanity there are so many different mental dispositions, that simply one religion, no matter how profound, cannot satisfy all the variety of people.

For instance, now, in spite of such a diversity of religious traditions, the majority of people still remain unattracted by religion. Of the five billion people, I believe only around one billion are true religious believers. While many people say, "My family background is Christian, Muslim or Buddhist, so I'm a Christian, Muslim or Buddhist," true believers, in their daily lives and particularly when some difficult situation arises, realize that they are followers of a particular religion. For example, I mean those who say, "I am Christian," and during that moment remember God, pray to God, and do not let out negative emotions. Of these true believers, I think there are perhaps less than one billion. The rest of humanity, four billion people, remain in the true sense non-believers. So one religion obviously cannot satisfy all of humanity. Under such circumstances, a variety of religions is actually necessary and useful, and therefore the only sensible thing is that all different

religions work together and live harmoniously, helping one another. There have been positive developments recently and I have noticed closer relations forming between various religions.

> **66 You should remember that these mental transformations take time and are not easy. 99**

Left, A procession of monks with a statue of Maitreya, the Buddha of the future, on the final day of the Monlam prayer festival, Tashikhyil Monastery, Amdo, Eastern Tibet.

So, having reflected upon the faults of a self-centered way of thinking and life, and also having reflected upon the positive consequences of being mindful of the well-being of other sentient beings and working for their benefit, and being convinced of this, then in Buddhist meditation there is a special training which is known as "the practice of Giving and Taking." This is especially designed to enhance your power of compassion and love toward other sentient beings. It basically involves visualizing taking upon yourself all the suffering, pain, negativity, and undesirable experiences of other sentient beings. You imagine taking these upon yourself and then giving away or sharing with others your own positive qualities, such as your virtuous states of mind, your positive energy, your wealth, your happiness, and so forth. Such a form of training, though it cannot actually result in a reduction of suffering by other sentient beings or a production of your own positive qualities, psychologically brings about a transformation in your mind so effectively that your feeling of love and compassion is much more enhanced.

Trying to implement this practice in your daily life is quite powerful and can be a very positive influence on your mind and on your health. If you feel that it seems worthwhile to practice, then irrespective of whether you are a believer or a non-believer, you should try to promote these basic human good qualities.

One thing you should remember is that these mental transformations take time and are not easy. I think some people from the West, where technology is so good, think that everything is automatic. You should not expect this spiritual transformation to take place within a short period; that is impossible. Keep it in your mind and make a constant effort, then after 1 year, 5 years, 10 years, 15 years, you will eventually find some change. I still sometimes find it very difficult to practice these things. However, I really do believe that these practices are extremely useful.

My favourite quotation from Shantideva's book is: "So long as sentient beings remain, so long as space remains, I will remain in order to serve, or in order to make some small contribution for the benefit of others."

Right, A wall painting of Shakyamuni Buddha making the mudra of explaining the teachings, Tashikhyil Monastery.

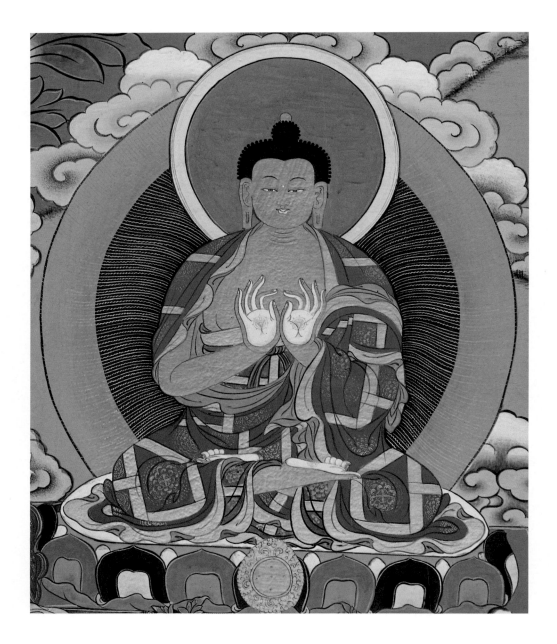

INTERDEPENDANCE, INTER-CONNECTEDNESS AND THE NATURE OF REALITY

> 66 **If we look at internal experiences, the past is no longer there and the future has not yet come: there is only the present.** 99

In a discussion of interdependence, inter-connectedness, and the nature of reality, the first question is: what is time? We cannot identify time as some sort of independent entity. Generally speaking, there are external matters and internal feelings or experiences. If we look at the external things, then generally there is the past, the present and the future. Yet if we look closely at "the present," such as the year, the month, the day, the hour, the minute, the second, we cannot find it. Just one second before the present is the past; and one second after is the future. There is no present. If there is no present, then it is difficult to talk about the past and the future, since both depend on the present. So if we look at external matters, it would seem that the past is just in our memory and the future is just in our imagination, nothing more than a vision.

Left, Monks playing musical instruments at a ceremony at Tashikhyil Monastery, Amdo, Eastern Tibet.

But if we look at our internal experiences or states of consciousness, the past is no longer there and the future has not yet come: there is only the present. So things become somewhat complicated when we think along these lines. This is the nature of interdependency, the Sanskrit word *pratityasamutpada.* This is a very useful idea and it is one of my favorite subjects.

There are two levels of interdependence: a conventional level and a deeper level. First I will deal with the conventional level. When we speak of the Buddhist principle of inter-dependence, which is often referred to as "interdependent origination," we must bear in mind that there are many different levels of understanding of that principle. The more superficial level of understanding of the principle is the interdependent nature or relationship between cause and effect. The deeper level of understanding of the principle is much more pervasive and, in fact, encompasses the entire spectrum of reality. The principle of interdependent origination in relation to cause and effect states that nothing can come about with-out the corresponding causes and conditions; everything comes into being as a result of an aggregation of causes and conditions.

If we consider the law of nature, we see it is not created by karma or by Buddha, it is just nature. We consider that Buddhahood developed according to natural law. Therefore, our experiences of pain and suffering, pleasure and joy, depend entirely on their own causes and conditions. Because of this natural relationship between causes and their effects, the Buddhist principle states that the less you desire a particular experience, event or phenomenon, the more effort you must put into preventing the aggregation of its causes and conditions, so that you can prevent the occurrence of

Right, His Holiness the Fourteenth Dalai Lama at a public teaching London, England, 1999.

Left, Monks at
Drepung Monastery
gazing out at the
Himalaya.

that event. And the more you desire a particular event, outcome or experience, the more attention you must pay to
ensure that these causes and conditions are accumulated so
that you can enjoy the outcome.

I personally believe that the relationship between a cause and
an effect is also a sort of natural law. I don't think that one
could come up with a rational explanation as to why effects
necessarily follow concordant causes and conditions. For
instance, it is stated that afflictive emotional states like anger
and hatred lead to undesirable consequences and, according to
the Buddhist scriptures, one consequence of hatred and anger
is ugliness. But there is not a full, rational account as to how
ugliness is a consequence of that particular afflictive emotion.
Yet in a way one can understand it, because when you experience very intense anger or hatred, even your facial expression
changes and you assume a very ugly face. Similarly, there are
certain types of mental and cognitive emotional states which
bring about almost instantaneous positive changes in your
facial expression. These states bring you presence of mind,
calmness, and serenity, and such an emotional state or thought
could lead to a more desirable outcome. So one can see a type
of connection, but not a full rational explanation.

But one might feel that there are certain types of emotional states, such as a very deep level of compassion, which are
positive, yet, when they occur within your mind, one might say
that at that particular instant there is no joy. For instance, a

person may be fully under the influence of compassion and therefore sharing the suffering of the object of compassion. In that case, one could argue, from what I have said earlier, that compassion cannot be said to be a positive cause. But here I think one must understand that, while it is true that as a result of compassion, because one is fully engaged in sharing the suffering of the object of compassion, at that instant there is a certain degree of pain, this is very different from a pain which is being suffered by someone who is depressed, desperate, and helpless, and feels a loss of hope. In the case of compassionate suffering, although the person is undergoing a sort of pain, there is definitely a high degree of alertness, and there is no loss of control because the person is, in a way, willingly taking on the suffering of the other person. So on the surface these emotional states might look as though they have a similar outcome, but they are entirely different. In one case, the

Above, A monk walking past the entrance to a prayer hall of Drepung Monastery, Tibet.

suffering is so overwhelming that the person has lost control and has given way to it, whereas in the case of compassion, the person is still in control of his or her thought.

❝ If you understand the interdependant relationship between cause and effect, you will appreciate the Four Noble Truths. ❞

Now if you understand the importance of appreciating the interdependent relationship between cause and effect, then you will appreciate the teachings on the Four Noble Truths. The entire teaching on the Four Noble Truths is based on the principle of causality. When the causal principle that is implied in these teachings is elaborated, you read Buddha's doctrine of the Twelve Links of Dependent Origination. In that teaching he stated that, because there is a particular cause, its effects follow; because the cause was created, the effect came about; and because there was ignorance, it led to action or karma.

So here you find three statements: one is that because the cause exists, the effect follows; because the cause was created, the effect was produced; and because there was ignorance, it led to the action. Now the first statement indicates that, from an affirmative point of view, when causes are aggregated, effects will naturally follow. And what is also implied in that statement is that it is due to the mere aggregation of the causes and conditions that the effects come into being, and that, apart from the causal process, there is no external power or force such as a Creator and so forth which brings these things into being.

The second statement again points out another important characteristic of dependent origination, which is that the very cause which brings about the effects must itself have a cause. If the cause is an eternally existing, permanent absolute entity, then such an entity could not be itself an effect of something else. If that is the case, then it will not have the potential to produce an effect. Therefore, first of all there must be a cause; second, that very cause must itself have a cause.

And the third statement points out another important characteristic of the principle of dependent origination. It is that the effect must be commensurate with the cause – there must be a concordance between the two. Not just anything can produce anything; there must be a sort of special relationship between cause and effect. Buddha gave an example of ignorance leading to action. Here the implication is, "Who commits that action?" It is a sentient being – and by committing an act motivated by an ignorant state of mind, that being is in a way accumulating his or her own downfall. Since there is no living being that desires unhappiness or suffering, it is due to ignorance that the individual engages in an act which has the potential to produce undesirable consequences.

Right, Ritual weapons, which symbolize the powers of the protective deities, are stacked beneath a wall painting of Ling Gesar, the epic hero of Tibetan Warriors, Tashikhyil Monastery.

Left, Pilgrims watch as monks perform a Sacred Cham dance, Tashikhyil Monastery, Amdo, Eastern Tibet.

So we find that all the Twelve Links of Dependent Origination fall into three classes of phenomena. First, there are afflictive emotions and thoughts; second, there is the karmic action and its imprints; and third, there is its effect: suffering. So the principal message is that suffering is something that we all do not desire, but it is a consequence or an effect of ignorance. Buddha did not state that suffering is an effect of consciousness, because if that was the case, then the process of liberation or the process of purification would necessarily involve putting an end to the very continuum of consciousness. One moral that we can draw from this teaching is that the sufferings which are rooted in afflictive and negative emotions and thoughts can be removed. This ignorant state of mind can be dispelled, because we can generate insight which perceives the nature of reality. So we see that the principle of dependent origination shows how all these twelve links in the chain of dependent origination which forms an individual's entry into the cycle of existence are inter-connected.

Now if we were to apply this inter-connectedness to our perception of reality as a whole, then we could generate a great insight from it. For instance, we would then be able to appreciate the interdependent nature of one's own and others' interests: how the interests and well-being of human beings is dependent upon the well-being of animals living on the same planet. Similarly, if we develop such an understanding of the nature of reality, we would also be able to appreciate the inter-connectedness between the well-being of human beings and the natural environment. We could also consider the present, the future, and so forth. We would then be able to cultivate an outlook on reality which is very holistic and has very significant implications.

66 **To have a happier future for oneself, you have to take care of everything that relates to you.** 99

So in a few words, you can see that there are no independent causes of one's own happiness. It depends on many other factors. So the conclusion is that in order to have a happier future for oneself, you have to take care of everything that relates to you. That is, I think, quite a useful view.

So far, I have spoken about the principle of dependent origination from the perspective of the first level of understanding. We can see in the Buddhist scriptures the importance of understanding this level of the dependent origination. In fact, one of the Mahayana texts known as, *the Compendium of Deeds*, in which Shantideva quotes heavily from Buddha's sutras, points out the need to first of all appreciate the inter-connectedness of all events and phenomena: how, due to the causal and

Left, A lay woman spinning a prayer wheel, Tashikhyil Monastery, Amdo, Eastern Tibet.

conditional process, phenomena and events come into being; and how crucial it is to respect that conventional reality, because it is at that level that we can understand how certain types of experiences lead to certain types of undesirable consequences, how certain causes, certain types of aggregation of causes and conditions can lead to more desirable consequences, and so forth; how, in fact, certain events can directly affect our well-being and experience. Because there is that sort of relationship, it is very crucial for practicing Buddhists to first develop a deep understanding of the perspective of the first level. Then Buddha states that one should go beyond that understanding and question the ultimate nature of the things that relate to each other in this inter-connected way. This points toward the Buddha's teachings on Emptiness.

In the teachings on the Twelve Links of Dependent Origination, the Buddha states that, although sentient beings do not desire suffering and dissatisfaction, it is through ignorance that they accumulate karmic actions which then lead to undesirable consequences. Now the question then is: what exactly is the nature of that ignorance? What is the mechanism that really leads an individual to act against what he or she fundamentally desires? Here Buddha points to the role of afflictive emotions and thoughts, like anger, hatred, attachment, and so forth, which blind the person's understanding of the nature of reality. If we were to examine the state of mind at the point when an individual experiences an intense emotion like hatred, anger or extreme attachment, we would find that, at that point, the person has a rather false notion of self: there is a kind of unquestioned assumption of an independently existing "I" or subject or person which is perceived, not necessarily consciously, as a kind of a master. It is not totally independent from the body or mind, nor is it to be identified with the body or mind, but there is something there which is somehow identified as the core of the being, the self, and there is a strong sort of grasping at that kind of identity or being. Based on that, you have strong emotional experiences, like attachment toward loved ones, or strong anger or hatred toward someone whom you perceive as threatening, and so forth.

Right, Monks walking down a hill after the Kalachakra Initiation ceremony officiated by His Holiness the Dalai Lama, Ki Monastery, Spiti, India.

66 **There is often a big disparity between the way in which we perceive things and the way things really are.** **99**

Similarly, if we were to examine how we really perceive our object of desire or object of anger, we would notice that there is a kind of assumption of an independently existing entity, something which is worthy of being desired or worthy of being hated. Aside from the subtle perspective of the doctrine of Emptiness, even in our day-to-day lives we often

find a disparity between the way we perceive things and the way things really exist. If that was not true, then the very idea of being deceived would not make sense. We often find ourselves totally disillusioned because we had false perceptions of reality. Once our illusion is dispelled, we realize that we have been deceived. So we often see in our own daily life cases where the appearance of something does not tally with the reality of the situation.

Similarly, as I pointed out in my talk on subtle impermanence, even from the perspective of the transient nature of phenomena there is often a big disparity between the way in which we perceive things and the way things really are. For instance, when we meet someone we say, "Oh, this is the very same person I've known for a long time." Again, when you see an object, you think, "Oh, this is the same object which I saw two days ago." This is a very crude way of talking about reality. What is actually happening here is a kind of a conflation between an image or a concept of an entity and the actual reality of the moment. In reality, the object or entity that we are perceiving has already gone through a lot of stages. It is dynamic, it is transient, it is momentary, so the object that we are perceiving now is never the same as the one which we perceived a day ago or two days ago, but we have the impression that we are perceiving the very same thing because what we are doing is conflating the concept of that object and the actual object. So we see again here a disparity between the way things appear to us and the way in which things really exist. Similarly, if we were to take the perspective of modern physics, then we would also find that there is a disparity between the common-sense view of reality and how scientists, from their point of view, would explain the nature of reality.

❝ The object that we are perceiving now is never the same as the one which we preceived a day ago ot two days ago. ❞

So what is clear from all this is the fact that there is some fault in our identification of an individual being as a self, as a person, or as an individual. But the question is: to what extent is it false? We cannot accept that the self or "I" does not exist at all, because if that is the case then a lot of our concerns, projects, and actions would not make any sense. Because of the fact that there is a self, our concerns for attaining full liberation for the sake of other sentient beings, our concern for the well-being of other sentient beings, becomes very serious, because there is someone or something who would either suffer or benefit as a result of the stand we adopt or actions we engage in. So the question really is: to what extent is our

Right, Monks wait on a hillside as a giant thangkha is carried through Sertang Monastery ready to be unfurled at dawn, Tagtsang Lhamo, Amdo, Eastern Tibet.

notion of self, our sense of identity, our understanding of the being or individual, false or deceived, and to what extent is it correct? Making the demarcation between the correct view of the self and person and the false view of the self and person is extremely difficult. It is because of this difficulty – yet at the same time the importance of being able to make such a distinction – that there emerged in India various Buddhist philosophical schools. Some schools only accept "identitylessness" of persons, but not of external events or phenomena; some schools accept the "identitylessness" of not only persons but also of the whole of existence, and even within that school there are various subtleties.

The reason why so much importance is placed on making the distinction is because it is so crucial to our attempt to liberate ourselves from suffering and its causes. This in part answers one of the questions that arose in one of the previous talks, that, if Buddhism accepts the doctrine of "no-self," what is it that takes rebirth?

We know that the doctrine of no-self or *anatman* is common to all the Buddhist schools of thought. The common doctrine of no-self is understood in terms of the denial of an independent and permanent self or soul. But what I will be presenting here is the understanding of Nagarjuna, as interpreted by the Indian pandit Chandrakirti. Nagarjuna, in his principal philosophical work, *The Fundamental Treatise on the Middle Way*, states that it is ignorance or misapprehension of the

Left, Monks walking past a large chorten (reliquary) at Sertang Monastery, Tagtsang Lhamo, Amdo, Eastern Tibet.

nature of reality which is at the root of our suffering. The manner in which one can attain liberation from suffering is by dispelling this ignorant state of mind, this misconceived notion of reality, by generating insight into the ultimate nature of reality. Nagarjuna identifies two types of ignorance: one is grasping at an inherent or intrinsic reality of one's own self or being; the other is grasping at an inherent and independent existence of external events and things. He goes on to state that this grasping at a "self" or "I" comes about as a result of grasping at our aggregates: our body, mind, and mental functions. He further states that the fact that we have to dispel this ignorance from within our minds, that we have to see through the misconception of our misapprehension, is clear. But simply by distancing ourselves from that grasping, simply by thinking that it is false, simply by thinking that it is destructive, and so on cannot ultimately help to free the individual from such forms of grasping. It is only by seeing through the illusion of that apprehension, it is only by generating an insight that would directly contradict the way in which, through that ignorance, we would normally perceive reality that we will be able to dispel that ignorance.

Right, A young monk seated outside reading a prayer book, Samye Monastery, Tibet.

An entity is composed of parts and there is a kind of necessary relationship between the whole and its parts.

Left, A procession
of monks playing
musical instruments
at a ceremony in
Tashikhyil
Monastery, Amdo,
Eastern Tibet.

So how do we go about seeing through the illusion of this false notion of self? How do we generate the insight that would directly contradict that form of perception? Nagarjuna says that if a "self," "I," or person exists as we normally assume it to exist, if it exists as we falsely view it, then the more we look for it, the more we search for its essence, the referent behind our terms and labels, then the clearer it should become. But that is not the case. If we were to search for the self or person as we normally perceive it, then it disappears, it sort of disintegrates, and this is an indication that such a notion of self was an illusion from the start. Because of this point, one of Nagarjuna's students, Aryadeva, stated in his *Four Hundred Verses on the Middle Way* that it is our ignorant conception or consciousness which is the seed of samsara (cyclic existence) and that things and events are its objects of grasping and apprehension. And it is only by seeing through the illusion of such a conception that we will be able to put an end to the process of existence.

We find in Nagarjuna's own writings extensive reasoning to refute the validity of our notion of self and negate the existence of self or person as we falsely perceive it. He argues that if the self or person is identical with the body, then just as the body is momentary, transient, changing every day, the self or the person should also be subject to the same law. For instance, a human being's bodily continuity can cease and, if the self is identical with the body, then the continuum of the self will also cease at that point. On the other hand, if the self is totally independent of the body, then how can it make sense to say, when a *person* is physically ill, that the person is ill, and so forth? Therefore, apart from the interrelationships between various factors that form our being, there is no independent self.

Similarly, if we extend the same analysis to external reality, we find that, for example, every material object has directional parts, certain parts facing toward different directions. We know that so long as it is an entity it is composed of parts and that there is a kind of necessary relationship between the whole and its parts, so we find that apart from the interrelationship between the various parts and the idea of wholeness, there is no independent entity existing outside that interface. We can apply the same analysis to consciousness or mental phenomena. Here the only difference is that the characteristics of consciousness or mental phenomena are not material or physical. However, we can analyze this in terms of the various instants or moments that form a continuum.

Since we cannot find the essence behind the label, or since we cannot find the referent behind the term, does it mean that nothing exists? The question could also be raised: is that absence of phenomena the meaning of the doctrine of Emptiness? Nagarjuna anticipates the criticism from the realists' perspective which argues that if phenomena do not exist as we perceive them, if phenomena cannot be found when

Right, A detail of a costume worn by a "gego" or discipline monk at a ceremony at Tashikhyil Monastery, Amdo, Eastern Tibet.

Left, Nuns perform a "kora" or circumambulation of Tashikhyil Monastery, Amdo, Eastern Tibet.

we search for their essence, then they do not exist. Therefore, a person or self would not exist. And if a person does not exist, then there is no action or karma because the very idea of karma involves someone committing the act; and if there is no karma, then there cannot be suffering because there is no experiencer, then there is no cause. And if that is the case, there is no possibility of freedom from suffering because there is nothing from which to be freed. Furthermore, there is no path that would lead to that freedom. And if that is the case, there cannot be a spiritual community or sangha that would embark on the path toward that liberation. And if that is the case, then there is no possibility of a fully perfected being or Buddha. So the realists argue that if Nagarjuna's thesis is true, that the essence of things cannot be found, then nothing will exist and one will have to deny the existence of samsara and Nirvana and everything.

66 The unfindability of phenomena when we search for their essence, indicates that phenomena lack intrinsic reality. 99

Nagarjuna says that such a criticism, that these consequences would follow from his thesis, indicates a lack of understanding of the subtle meaning of the doctrine of Emptiness, because the doctrine of Emptiness does not state or imply the non-existence of everything. Also the doctrine of Emptiness is not simply the thesis that things cannot be found when we search for their essence. The meaning of Emptiness is the interdependent nature of reality.

Nagarjuna goes on to say what he means by the claim that the true meaning of Emptiness emerges from an understanding of the principle of dependent origination. He states that because phenomena are dependent originations, because phenomena come about as a result of interdependent relationships between causes and conditions, they are empty. They are empty of inherent and independent status. An appreciation of that view is an understanding of the true Middle Way. In other words, when we understand dependent origination, we see that not only the existence of phenomena, but also the identity of phenomena, depend upon other factors.

So dependent origination can dispel extremes of both absolutism and nihilism, because the idea of "dependence" points toward a form of existence which lacks independent or absolute status, therefore it liberates the individual from extremes of absolutism. In addition, "origination" frees the individual from falling to the extremes of nihilism, because origination points toward an understanding of existence, that things do exist.

I stated earlier that the unfindability of phenomena or entities when we search for their essence is not really a full meaning of Emptiness, but at the same time it indicates that phenomena lack intrinsic reality, they lack independent and inherent existence. What is meant by this is that their existence and their identity are derived from mere interaction of various factors. Buddhapalita, one of the disciples of Nagarjuna, states that because phenomena come about due to the interaction of various factors, their very existence and identity are derived from other factors. Otherwise, if they had independent existence, if they possessed intrinsic reality, then there would be no need for them to be dependent on other factors. The very fact that they depend on other factors is an indication that they lack independent or absolute status.

So the full understanding of Emptiness can come about only when one appreciates the subtlety of this principle of dependent origination – if one concludes that the ultimate nature is that phenomena cannot be found if we were to search for their essence. Nagarjuna states that if the principle or doctrine of Emptiness is not valid, if phenomena are not devoid of independent and inherent existence and intrinsic reality, then they will be absolute; therefore there will be no room for the principle of dependent origination to operate and there will be no room for the interdependent principle to operate. If that is the case, it would not be possible for causal principles to operate and therefore the holistic perception of reality also becomes a false notion. And if that is so, then the whole idea of the Four Noble Truths will be invalid because there is no causal principle operating. Then you will be denying the entire teachings of the Buddha.

In fact, what Nagarjuna does is to reverse all the criticisms levelled against his thesis, by stating that in the realists' position all the teachings of the Buddha would have to be denied. He sums up his criticism by saying that any system of belief or practice which denies the doctrine of Emptiness can explain nothing coherently, whereas any system of belief or thought which accepts this principle of interdependent origination, this doctrine of Emptiness, can come up with a coherent account of reality.

Right, Prayer flags fluttering in the wind on the Pang La Pass with a view of Mount Everest in the background, Tibet.

66 As your insight into the ultimate nature of reality is deepened, you will perceive phenomena as illusion-like. 99

So what we find here is a very interesting complementary relationship between the two levels of understanding of dependent origination I spoke of earlier. The perspective of the

first level really accounts for much of our everyday existence or everyday world of experience, where causes and conditions interact and there is a causal principle operating. That perspective of dependent origination, according to Buddhism, is called the correct view at the worldly level. The greater your appreciation of that perspective, the closer you will be able to come to the deeper level of understanding of dependent origination, because your understanding of the causal mechanism at that level is used to arrive at an understanding of the empty nature of all phenomena. Similarly, once your insight into the empty nature of all phenomena becomes deep, then your conviction in the efficacy of causes and effects will be strengthened, so there will be a greater respect for the conventional reality and the relative world. So there is a kind of interesting complementary relationship between the two perspectives.

As your insight into the ultimate nature of reality and Emptiness is deepened and enhanced, you will develop a perception of reality from which you will perceive phenomena and events as sort of illusory, illusion-like, and this mode of perceiving reality will permeate all your interactions with reality. Consequently, when you come across a situation in which you generate compassion, instead of becoming more detached from the object of compassion, your engagement will be deeper and fuller. This is because compassion is ultimately founded upon a valid mode of thought and you will have gained a deeper insight into the nature of reality.

Left, A senior lama presiding at a prayer ceremony, Tashikhyil Monastery, Amdo, Eastern Tibet.

Conversely, when you confront situations which would normally give rise to afflictive, negative emotions and responses on your part, there will be a certain degree of detachment and you will not fall prey to the influences of those negative and afflictive emotions. This is because, underlying those afflictive emotions and thoughts, such as desire, hatred, anger, and so forth, there is a mistaken notion of reality, which involves grasping at things as absolute, independent, and unitary. When you generate insight into Emptiness, the grip of these emotions on your mind will be loosened.

At the beginning of my talk I gave an example of our concept of time: ordinarily we presume there is a kind of an independent existent or independent entity called "time" present or past or future. But when we examine it at a deeper level, we find it is a mere convention. Other than the interface between the three tenses, the present, future, and past, there is no such thing as an independently existing present moment, so we generate a sort of dynamic view of reality. Similarly, when I think of myself, although initially I might have an unquestioned assumption of there being an independent self, when I look closer I will find that, apart from the interface of various factors that constitute my being and various moments of the continuum that form my being, there is no such thing as an absolute independent entity. Since it is this mere conventional "self," "I" or person that goes toward the

Right, A "gego" or discipline monk watching over a prayer ceremony, Tashikhyil Monastery, Amdo, Eastern Tibet.

attainment of liberation or eventually transforms into Buddha, even Buddha is not absolute.

There is a similar case with the phenomenon mentioned earlier, the idea of Clear Light, which is the most subtle level of consciousness. Again, one should not conceive of it as some kind of independently existing entity. Apart from the continuum of consciousness which forms this phenomenon called Clear Light, we cannot speak of an independently existing absolute entity.

66 **When we examine the nature of reality we find it is empty of inherent existence.** 99

Likewise, we will find that many of our concepts indicate a very deep, very complex inter-connectedness. For instance, when we speak of ourselves as subjects, we can make sense of that notion only in relation to an object – the idea of a subject makes sense only in relation to an object. Similarly, the idea of action makes sense in relation to a being, an agent who commits the act. So if we were to analyze a lot of these concepts, we would find we cannot really separate the entity or the phenomenon from its context.

Again, if we go beyond the idea that things are mere designations or labels and ask whose conceptual thought creates the labels, whether it is the past conception or the future conception, whether it is the conception of a particular being or the collective conception, and so forth, we will not find an independent existence.

Even Emptiness itself, which is seen as the ultimate nature of reality, is not absolute, nor does it exist independently. We cannot conceive of Emptiness as independent of a basis of phenomena, because when we examine the nature of reality we find that it is empty of inherent existence. Then if we are to take that Emptiness itself as an object and look for its essence, again we will find that it is empty of inherent existence. Therefore Buddha taught the Emptiness of Emptiness. However, when we search for the true essence of a phenomenon or event, what we find is this Emptiness. But that does not mean that Emptiness itself is absolute, because Emptiness as a concept or as an entity cannot withstand this analysis. If we were to take Emptiness itself as an object and then again examine it, we cannot find it. However, in some scriptures we will find references to Emptiness as ultimate truth. Here one should understand what is the meaning of this term "ultimate." One should not mistake it in terms of Emptiness as being ultimately true, or absolute, but rather it is called "ultimate truth" because it is an object of the insight that has penetrated into the nature of reality.

THE CHALLENGE FOR HUMANITY: AN INTERFAITH ADDRESS

Left, Young monks above a large thangka of Yama Dharmaraja, the black buffalo-headed "Lord of the Dead", Tashikhyil Monastery.

We have seen in this present age tremendous advances in the field of material development. As a result, there has been a marked improvement in the lives of human beings. Yet, at the same time, we are also aware that material development alone cannot answer all of humanity's dreams. Moreover, as material development reaches a higher and higher stage, we sometimes find that it brings with it certain complications, including more problems and challenges for us. Because of this fact, I think that all the major religious traditions of the world have the potential to contribute to the benefit and well-being of humanity, and also that they retain their relevance in the modern age.

However, since many of these major world religions evolved a long time ago in human history, I am quite sure that many aspects of their religious teachings and traditions reflect the needs and concerns of different times and cultures. Therefore, I think it is quite important to be able to make a distinction between what I call the "core" and "essence" of religious teachings and the cultural aspects of the particular tradition. What I would call the "essence" or "core" of religious traditions are the basic religious messages, such as the principles of love, compassion, and so forth, which always retain their relevance and importance, irrespective of time and circumstances. But as time changes, the cultural context changes, and I think it is important for the followers of religious traditions to be able to make the necessary changes that would reflect the particular concerns of their time and culture.

> **66** If one's faith remains only at the intellectual level, then I think that is a grave mistake. **99**

I think the most important task of any religious practitioner is to examine oneself within one's own mind and try to transform one's body, speech, and mind, and act according to the teachings and the principles of the religious tradition that one is following. This is very important. Conversely, if one's faith or practice of religion remains only at the intellectual level of knowledge, such as being familiar with certain doctrines without translating them into one's behavior or conduct, then I think that is a grave mistake. In fact, if someone possesses certain intellectual knowledge of religious traditions or teachings, yet his or her consciousness and mental continuum remain totally uninfluenced by it, then this could be quite destructive. It could lead to a situation in which the person, because of having the knowledge of the religious beliefs, could use the religion for the purposes of exploitation and manipulation. So, I think, as practitioners, our first responsibility is to watch ourselves.

The situation of today's world is completely different from the past. In the past, human communities and societies remained more or less independent of one another. Under such

Right, Young monks at a ceremony at Tashikhyil Monastery, Amdo, Eastern Tibet.

circumstances, ideas of a single religion, a monolithic culture, and so forth, made sense and had a place in the cultural context. But this situation has now completely changed as a result of various factors: easy access between various countries, an information revolution, easy transportation, and so forth. So human society can no longer function on that model.

Let us take as an example the city of London. London is a city which is multi-cultural and has multiple religions. Therefore, if we don't exercise caution and utilize our intelligence, there is a possibility of conflict based on divergent religious beliefs and cultures. So it is very important to have an outlook that takes into account the existence of multiple religions, the plurality of religions. The best way to meet this challenge is not just to study other religious traditions through reading books, but more importantly to meet with people from other religious traditions so that you can share experiences with them and learn from their experiences. Through personal contact you will be able to really appreciate the value of other religious traditions.

From a wider perspective, there are definitely strong grounds for appreciating pluralism in religion and culture, particularly in religion. It is a fact that among humanity there are many diverse mental dispositions, interests, needs, and so on. Therefore, the greater the diversity of religious traditions that are available, the greater their capacity to meet the needs of different people.

Left, Monks on their way to a ceremony before dawn at Sertang Monastery, Tagtsang Lhamo, Amdo, Eastern Tibet.

In the history of humanity there have been very tragic events which came about because of religion. Even to this day, we see that conflicts arise in the name of religion and the human community is further divided. If we were to meet this challenge, then I am sure we would find that there are enough grounds on which we can build harmony between the various religions and develop a genuine respect toward each other.

Another important challenge facing hu-manity now is the issue of environmental protection. In fact, a number of prominent environmentalists have expressed their wish to see more active initiatives taken by the different religious traditions and especially by their leaders. I think this is a wish that is very valid. Personally, I feel that much of the environmental problem really stems from our insatiable desire, lack of contentment, and greed. It is in the religious teachings that we find various instructions that enable us to keep a check on our desires and greed, and to positively transform our behavior and conduct. Therefore, I think religious traditions have not only a potential but also a great responsibility to make contributions in that direction.

Another thing that I consider very important, and which is a responsibility that religious traditions must take upon themselves, is the putting forward of a united front against war and conflict. I know that in human history there have been a few cases where, through war, freedom has been won and certain goals have been achieved. But I personally believe that war cannot ever lead to the ultimate solution of a problem. Therefore, I think it is important for all the religious traditions to take a united stand and voice their opposition to the very idea of war. But voicing one's opposition to war alone is not enough. We must do something to bring about an end to war and conflict, and one of the things that we have to seriously think about is the question of disarmament. I know that the motivating factor which triggers the need for weapons is human emotion – hatred and anger. But there is no way that we can completely eliminate anger and hatred from the minds of human beings. We can definitely reduce their force and alleviate them, but not completely eliminate them. That means that we have to make serious efforts to achieve disarmament.

Another challenge that we face is the question of population. I know that from the point of view of all religious traditions, life, human life in particular, is precious. From the viewpoint of individual human beings, the more humans there are the better it is, because then we have the opportunity for more human lives to come into being. However, if we look at this issue from a global perspective, then I think there is definitely a need for all religious traditions to give the population issue very serious thought, because the world's resources are limited. There is only a certain degree to which world resources can sustain human beings on this planet.

Right, Silhouette of His Holiness the Dalai Lama, Ki Monastery, Spiti, India.

GLOSSARY

Abhidharmakosha (Treasury of Knowledge) by Vasubandhu. English translation (from a French translation) by Leo M. Pruden,

Abhidharmakoshabhashyam, Berkeley, California, Asian Humanities Press, 1991.

Abhidharmasamuchchaya – see Compendium of Knowledge

Arhat (Tib. dgra bcom pa) – to become an Arhat is the final goal of the Shravakayana. It is a form of nirvana, beyond rebirth, but falls short of buddhahood. The Tibetan word literally means "one who has subdued the enemies", i.e. negative emotions.

Aryadeva – a disciple of Nagarjuna and author of many important commentaries.

Asanga – great Indian master, half-brother of Vasubandhu, who composed important Mahayana works inspired by Maitreya. He is especially known as a proponent of the Chittamatra school. Circa 4th century.

Bhavaviveka – also known as Bhavya, the key figure in the development of Svatantrika-Madhyamaka.

Bodhicharyavatara – see Guide to the Bodhisattva's Way of Life.

Bodhisattva – a being who has decided to bring all beings to enlightenment and who is practicing the Bodhisattva path of the Mahayana.

Buddhapalita – circa 4th century Indian master, founder of Prasangika-Madhyamaka.

Chandrakirti – circa 3–4th century master, the greatest figure in the Prasangika-Madhyamaka school.

Chatuhshatakashastrakarika – see Four Hundred Verses on the Middle Way

Clear Words (abbreviated Skt. title: Prasannapada; full title: Mulamadhyamakavrttiprasannapada) – a commentary by Chandrakirti on Nagarjuna's Mulamadhyamikakarika. English translation of selected chapters in M. Sprung, "Lucid Exposition of the Middle Way".

Commentary on the Compendium of Valid Cognition (Pramanavarttikakarika) by Dharma-kirti. No English translation.

Compendium of Knowledge (Abhidharmasa-muchchaya) by Asanga. French translation by Walpola Rahula, **Le Compendium de la Super- Doctrine (Philosophie d'Asanga)**, Paris, Ecole Française d'Extrême-Orient, 1971.

Dharmakirti – famous Buddhist master of the 7th century.

Emptiness (Skt. shunyata) – the absence of true existence in all phenomena.

Enlightenment (Skt. bodhi) – purification of all obscurations and realization of all qualities.

Four Hundred Verses on the Middle Way (Chatuhshatakashastrakarika) by Aryadeva. English translations by K. Lang, **Aryadeva's Chatuhshataka: On the Bodhisattva's Cultivation of Merit and Knowledge**, Indiske Studier, Vol. VII, Copenhagen, Akademish Forlag, 1986; and Geshe Sonam Rinchen and Ruth Sonam, **Yogic Deeds of Bodhisattvas: Gyelstap on**

Aryadeva's Four Hundred, Ithaca, Snow Lion, 1994.

Fundamentals of the Middle Way (Mulamadhyamikakarika) – a seminal text by Nagarjuna. English translation by F. Streng, **Emptiness: A Study in Religious Meaning**, Nashville and New York, Abingdon Press, 1967. See also K. Inada, **Nagarjuna: A Translation of his Mulamadhyamikakarika**, Tokyo, Hokuseido Press, 1970.

Guide to the Bodhisattva's Way of Life (Bodhicharyavatara) by Shantideva. English translations include A **Guide to the Bodhisattva's Way of Life** by Stephen Batchelor, Dharamsala, Library of Tibetan Works and Archives, 1979; and **The Way of the Bodhisattra**, translated by the Padmakara Translation Group, Shambhala, Boston, 1997.

Liberation (skt. moksha) – freedom from samsara, either as an arhat or as a buddha. Madhyamaka – literally "the middle way". The highest of the four main Buddhist schools of philosophy. First expounded by Nagarjuna and considered to be the basis of Vajrayana. The Middle Way means not holding to any extreme views, especially those of eternalism and nihilism.

Mahayana – literally "the Great Vehicle", the vehicle of bodhisattvas. It is great because it aims at full buddhahood for the sake of all beings.

Maitreya – the Buddha to come, the fifth in this present cosmic age. Many Mahayana teachings were inspired by Maitreya.

Mandala – the universe with the palace of a deity in the centre, as described in the Tantric practice of visualization.

Mantra – manifestation of supreme enlightenment in the form of sound. Syllables used in Tantric visualization practices to invoke the wisdom deities.

Mulamadhyamikakarika – see Fundamentals of the Middle Way

Nagarjuna – Indian master of 1st–2nd century CE who expounded the teachings of Madhyamaka, and composed numerous philosophical treatises.

Path of accumulation – the first of the five paths according to Mahayana. On this path one accumulates the causes that will make it possible to proceed towards enlightenment.

Path of connection – the second of the five paths according to Mahayana. On this path one connects oneself to, or prepares oneself for, seeing the two kinds of absence of self.

Path of seeing – the third of the five paths according to Mahayana. It is called this because one really sees the two kinds of absence of self, that of the individual and that of phenomena.

Pramanavarttikakarika – see Commentary on the Compendium of Valid Cognition

Prasannapada – see Clear Words

Samsara – the cycle of unenlightened existence in which one is endlessly propelled by negative emotions and karma from one state of rebirth to another. The root of samsara is ignorance.

Shamatha – "calm abiding". The meditative practice of calming the mind in order to rest free from the disturbance of thought.

Shantideva – great Indian poet and master of the 7th century C.E.

Shravaka – follower of the root vehicle of Buddhism (Shravakayana)

whose goal is to attain liberation from the suffering of samsara as an arhat. Unlike bodhisattvas, shravakas do not aspire to attain enlightenment for the sake of all beings.

Shravakayana – the vehicle of the hearers or listeners, based on the teachings of the Four Noble Truths.

Sutra – the teachings of both the Shravakayana and the Mahayana.

Uttaratantra – the full Sanskrit title is Mahayana-uttaratantrashastra (Supreme Continuum of the Mahayana). This text is ascribed to Maitreya. English translations from the Sanskrit by E. Obermiller, **Sublime Science of the Great Vehicle to Salvation in Acta Orientalia** 9 (1931), pp. 81–306; and J. Takasaki, **A Study on the Ratnagotravibhaga**, Rome, ISMEO, 1966. English translation from the Tibetan by Ken and Katia Holmes, The Changeless Nature, Dumfriesshire, Karma Drubgyud Darjay Ling, 1985.

Vajrayana – literally "the diamond vehicle", also known as Tantrayana.

Vasubandhu – great Indian master, brother of Asanga, who composed classic philosophical works on the Sarvastivada, Sautrantika and Chittamatra doctrines.

Vipashyana – clear insight meditation.

NOTES

INTRODUCTION

1.   Dependent origination, or dependent arising, are translations of the Sanskrit *pratitya samutpada*. It is the natural law that all phenomena arise "dependent upon" their own causes "in connection with" their individual conditions. Everything arises exclusively due to and dependent upon the coincidence of causes and conditions without which they cannot possibly appear.

2.   A buddha is literally someone who is awakened (from Sanskrit *bodhi*, awake) so buddhahood is the awakened state.

3.   "Cessation" is a technical term meaning 'the complete cessation of suffering'. Samsara refers to the cycle of suffering, and the cessation of that cycle is commonly identified as nirvana.

4.   See *Majjhima Nikaya I*, p. 190–191, Pali Text Society. See also the *Pratityamutpada Sutra*.

CHAPTER ONE

1. The Changeless Nature, translation of the *Uttaratantra* by Ken and Katia Holmes, Karma Drubgyud Darjay Ling, UK, 1985. Page 135. The *Uttaratantra* is also known as the *Ratnagotravibhaga*.

2. The Twelve Links of Dependent Origination form the twelvefold cycle of causal connections which binds beings to samsaric existence and thus perpetuates suffering. These Links are depicted around the famous Buddhist Wheel of Life, which illustrates the six realms of samsara and their various causes. The Links are, going clockwise around the Wheel: ignorance, volition or karmic formations, consciousness, name and form, the six bases of consciousness, contact, feeling, desire, attachment, becoming, birth, and old age and death. See *The Meaning of Life from a Buddhist Perspective* by His Holiness the Dalai Lama, translated and edited by Jeffrey Hopkins, Wisdom Publications, 1992.

CHAPTER TWO

1. For a detailed treatment of Buddhist cosmology in English, see *Myriad Worlds* by Jamgon Kongtrul, Snow Lion, 1995.

2. The human world is part of the Desire Realm. The Formless Realm is more subtle than the Form Realm, which in turn is more subtle than the Desire Realm.

3.   The early teachings of Buddhism are divided into the Vinaya, or code of discipline, the Sutras, or discourses of the Buddha, and the Abhidharma which is the commentarial and philosophical literature composed by Buddhist masters. Two complete corpuses of Abhidharma literature have survived to the present day: that of the Theravada school, in Pali, and that of the Sarvastivada school, in Sanskrit. Only the Sarvastivadin Abhidharma was taught in Tibet. The chief reference on cosmology is Chapter Three of Vasubandhu's *Abhidharmakosha*, translated into English by Leo Pruden, Asian Humanities Press, Berkeley California, 1991.

4.   Three Aspects of the Path, verse 7. See Robert Thurman's *Life and Teachings of Tsongkhapa,* Library of Tibetan Works and Archives, Dharamsala, India, 1982.

5.   According to Tibetan Buddhism there are six realms in samsara, each dominated by a particular mental poison. They are: the hell realms (anger), the animal realm (ignorance), the realm of pretas or hungry ghosts (miserliness), the human realm (desire), the demi-god or Asura realm (jealousy), and the god realm (pride).

6.   This statement can be found in *Majjhima Nikaya I* (p. 262, Pali Text Society) and *Majjhima III* (p. 43, Pali Text Society) and *Samyutta Nikaya II* (p. 28, Pali Text Society).

7.   Buddhist psychology bases the perception process on six sense faculties: sight, hearing, smell, taste, touch and thought. Each faculty relates to a sense organ (eye, ear, nose, tongue, body, mind) and to a consciousness which functions specifically with that organ. There are thus six sense consciousnesses, the sixth one being the mental consciousness.

CHAPTER THREE

1.   The term "karma" comes from the Sanskrit word "karman", meaning 'action'. It has three main meanings in Indian philosophy. The first is karma as ritual action, namely the sacrifice, in the early Vedas and Mimamsa philosophy. The second is karma as a particular category of human action, namely defiled and limited action, which we find in Samkhya Yoga, Advaita, the Bhagavad Gita and Buddhism. And the third meaning refers to karma not as an action but as a theory of action, in particular the theory of action as causal determinant. It is to this third meaning that the Dalai Lama refers here.

2.   *Chatuhshatakashastrakarika*, chapter 8, verse 15.

3.   See in particular the third and fourth chapters in Vasubandhu's *Abhidharmakosha*.

4.   See a fuller discussion of this topic by His Holiness the Dalai Lama in dialogue with David Bohm in *Dialogues with Scientists and Sages: The Search for Unity*, edited by Renée Weber (Routledge and Kegan Paul, London, 1986).

CHAPTER FOUR

1.   The third category of phenomena are "very obscure phenomena", which are beyond ordinary direct perception and logical inference. Generally, they can only be established on the basis of another's testimony or through scriptural authority.

2.   This view is held in particular by the Shravakayana schools, especially the Vaibhasikas or Sarvastivadins, and the Sautrantikas.

3.   Chapter XXIV, verse 18.

4.   His Holiness is referring to a text known as *The Interwoven Praise* (sPal mar bstod pa), which is a commentary in verse on Tsongkhapa's famous *Praise to the Buddha for his teachings on Dependent Origination* (rTen 'brel bstod pa). Lodrö Gyatso was a late nineteenth century Gelug master from Amdo and was more widely known as Chone Lama Rinpoche.

CHAPTER FIVE

1.　See the *Dasabhumika Sutra* for an explanation of the stages of the bodhisattva path.

2.　In the Indian tradition, the Buddhist path was generally presented as the Noble Eightfold Path, which is composed of: right view, right intention, right speech, right action, right livelihood, right effort, right meditation, and right concentration. The Tibetan tradition also describes the Buddhist path in terms of the Five Paths, which are the path of accumulation, the path of connection, the path of seeing, the path of meditation, and the path of no more learning. Within this framework, the Noble Eightfold Path would be included in the path of meditation.

3.　The Bodhicharyavatara by Shantideva, X.55.